# NEW INTERNATIO
# BIBLICAL COMMEN1

*New Testament Editor,*
W. Ward Gasque

# GALATIANS

*post*
Ref.
225.7
N418
V.9

*New Testament Series*

# NEW INTERNATIONAL BIBLICAL COMMENTARY

# GALATIANS

# L. ANN JERVIS

Based on the New International Version

© 1999 by Hendrickson Publishers, Inc.
P. O. Box 3473
Peabody, Massachusetts 01961–3473

First published jointly, 1999, in the United States by
Hendrickson Publishers and in the United Kingdom by the
Paternoster Press, P. O. Box 300, Carlisle, Cumbria CA3 0QS.
All rights reserved.

*Printed in the United States of America*

*First printing — November 1999*

**Library of Congress Cataloging-in-Publication Data**

Jervis, L. Ann.
   Galatians  /  L. Ann Jervis.
     (New International biblical commentary; 9. New
Testament series)
   "Based on the New International Version."
   Includes bibliographical references and indexes.
   1. Bible.  N.T.  Galatians—Commentaries.  I. Title.
II. Series: New International biblical commentary; 9.
  BS2685.3.J47   1999
  227'.4077—dc21                     99–40848
                                           CIP

ISBN 1–56563–007–6 (U.S. softcover)
ISBN 1–56563–506–X (U.S. hardcover)

**British Library Cataloguing in Publication Data**
**A catalogue record for this book is available**
**from the British Library.**

ISBN 0–85364–663–5 (U.K. softcover)

To Dylan Michael
and Bronwyn Leigh

# Table of Contents

## Foreword
## New International Biblical Commentary

Although it does not appear on the standard best-seller lists, the Bible continues to outsell all other books. And in spite of growing secularism in the West, there are no signs that interest in its message is abating. Quite to the contrary, more and more men and women are turning to its pages for insight and guidance in the midst of the ever-increasing complexity of modern life.

This renewed interest in Scripture is found both outside and inside the church. It is found among people in Asia and Africa as well as in Europe and North America; indeed, as one moves outside of the traditionally Christian countries, interest in the Bible seems to quicken. Believers associated with the traditional Catholic and Protestant churches manifest the same eagerness for the Word that is found in the newer evangelical churches and fellowships.

We wish to encourage and, indeed, strengthen this worldwide movement of lay Bible study by offering this new commentary series. Although we hope that pastors and teachers will find these volumes helpful in both understanding and communicating the Word of God, we do not write primarily for them. Our aim is to provide for the benefit of every Bible reader reliable guides to the books of the Bible—representing the best of contemporary scholarship presented in a form that does not require formal theological education to understand.

The conviction of editor and authors alike is that the Bible belongs to the people and not merely to the academy. The message of the Bible is too important to be locked up in erudite and esoteric essays and monographs written only for the eyes of theological specialists. Although exact scholarship has its place in the service of Christ, those who share in the teaching office of the church have a responsibility to make the results of their research accessible to the Christian community at large. Thus, the Bible scholars who join in the presentation of this series write with these broader concerns in view.

A wide range of modern translations is available to the contemporary Bible student. Most of them are very good and much to be preferred—for understanding, if not always for beauty—to the older King James Version (the so-called Authorized Version of the Bible). The Revised Standard Version has become the standard English translation in many seminaries and colleges and represents the best of modern Protestant scholarship. It is also available in a slightly altered "common Bible" edition with the Catholic imprimatur, and the New Revised Standard Version appeared in 1989. In addition, the New American Bible is a fresh translation that represents the best of post-Vatican II Roman Catholic biblical scholarship and is in a more contemporary idiom than that of the RSV.

The New Jerusalem Bible, based on the work of French Catholic scholars but vividly rendered into English by a team of British translators, is perhaps the most literary of the recent translations, while the New English Bible is a monument to modern British Protestant research. The Good News Bible is probably the most accessible translation for the person who has little exposure to the Christian tradition or who speaks and reads English as a second language. Each of these is, in its own way, excellent and will be consulted with profit by the serious student of Scripture. Perhaps most will wish to have several versions to read, both for variety and for clarity of understanding—though it should be pointed out that no one of them is by any means flawless or to be received as the last word on any given point. Otherwise, there would be no need for a commentary series like this one!

We have chosen to use the New International Version as the basis for this series, not because it is necessarily the best translation available but because it is becoming increasingly used by lay Bible students and pastors. It is the product of an international team of "evangelical" Bible scholars who have sought to translate the Hebrew and Greek documents of the original into "clear and natural English . . . idiomatic [and] . . . contemporary but not dated," suitable for "young and old, highly educated and less well educated, ministers and laymen [*sic*]." As the translators themselves confess in their preface, this version is not perfect. However, it is as good as any of the others mentioned above and more popular than most of them.

Each volume will contain an introductory chapter detailing the background of the book and its author, important themes, and other helpful information. Then, each section of the book will be expounded as a whole, accompanied by a series of notes on items in the text that need further clarification or more detailed explanation. Appended to the end of each volume will be a bibliographical guide for further study.

Our new series is offered with the prayer that it may be an instrument of authentic renewal and advancement in the worldwide Christian community and a means of commending the faith of the people who lived in biblical times and of those who seek to live by the Bible today.

W. WARD GASQUE

# Abbreviations

| | |
|---|---|
| AB | Anchor Bible |
| *ABD* | *Anchor Bible Dictionary* |
| AnBib | Analecta Biblica |
| *ANF* | *Ante-Nicene Fathers* |
| *ANRW* | *Aufstieg und Niedergang der römischen Welt* |
| *Ant.* | Josephus, *Antiquities* |
| BAGD | Bauer, Arndt, Gingrich, and Danker, *Greek-English Lexicon of the New Testament and Other Early Christian Literature* |
| *CBQ* | *Catholic Biblical Quarterly* |
| *Dial.* | Justin Martyr, *Dialogue with Trypho* |
| *Eth. nic.* | Aristotle, *Nicomachean Ethics* |
| *Good Person* | Philo, *That Every Good Person Is Free* |
| *Hist.* | Tacitus, *Historiae (Histories)* |
| *HTR* | *Harvard Theological Review* |
| *JBL* | *Journal of Biblical Literature* |
| *Jub.* | *Jubilees* |
| LCL | Loeb Classical Library |
| lit. | literally |
| Macc. | Maccabees |
| NEB | New English Bible |
| NIV | New International Version |
| *NovT* | *Novum Testamentum* |
| NovTSup | Novum Testamentum Supplement |
| NT | New Testament |
| *NTS* | *New Testament Studies* |
| OT | Old Testament |
| *Pol.* | Aristotle, *Politics* |
| SBLSBS | Society of Biblical Literature Sources for Biblical Study |
| SBLSP | Society of Biblical Literature Seminar Papers |
| SBT | Studies in Biblical Theology |
| *SJT* | *Scottish Journal of Theology* |

| | |
|---|---|
| SNTSMS | Society for New Testament Studies: Monograph Series |
| *t.* | *Tosefta* |
| *War* | Josephus, *Jewish War* |
| WBC | Word Biblical Commentary |

# Introduction

Paul's letter to the Galatian churches is one of the most riveting and personal and rich of the apostle's writings. It is riveting because we hear Paul reaching out to what he regards as a crisis situation with the only thing at his disposal—his words. It is personal because Paul exposes his profound feelings for the Galatian believers and reveals the depth of his convictions about the correctness of his gospel. It is rich because, in the course of seeking to persuade the Galatian believers that there is no other way to be children of God than the one they had accepted from him, Paul gives startling, provocative, and creative interpretations of Scripture. He describes his relationship with the Jerusalem church; his general moral outlook; something of his understanding of the dynamic that now exists between the law, justification, and being "in Christ"; and the centrality of the crucified Christ to his faith. In a blunt and urgent style Paul addresses matters that have relevance even for readers living in different circumstances nearly two thousand years later.

## The Situation That Provoked the Writing of Galatians

Today's readers of Galatians can sense Paul's attachment to the Galatian believers. His preaching of the gospel to them was in the context of a developing personal relationship. He says that he first preached the gospel "because of an illness" (4:13). During Paul's illness the Galatians treated him with care and dignity, and this beginning to Paul's relationship with them developed into a tender, honest, and privileged one in which, even in the face of their rejection of his gospel, Paul can address his readers as "my dear children" (4:19) and speak with utmost frankness. Paul writes because he wants to protect his gospel and because he cares deeply about the Galatian believers.

At the outset, Paul states that he thinks the Galatian believers are in danger of turning away from God and heeding another gospel (1:6). As we read the letter we see how dangerous Paul considers such a move, how sensible it must have seemed to the Galatian believers, and how personally attached Paul feels to Christ, to the Galatians, and to the gospel he proclaims.

Paul thinks that a move away from the gospel he preaches is perilous first because his gospel is the only gospel. Its singular truth came to him through revelation (1:12) and dramatically changed the focus of his life (1:13–16), as it did that of the Galatians (3:1–5). Second, a move away from his gospel is dangerous because it is a move away from freedom (5:1) and from the privileges that accrue to faith (3:29–4:7). Third, to move away from his gospel is to move away from Christ (5:2–4), for Paul identifies his gospel with Christ (1:16). Faith in the gospel is faith in Christ, which is why Paul can equate the coming of faith with the coming of Christ (3:23–25).

As Paul seeks to convince his readers not to be persuaded by those he describes as confusers and agitators (1:7; 5:10; 5:12), it becomes evident that to the Galatians his opponents had a convincing and appealing point of view. It seems that the gospel preached by Paul's rivals had two main advantages over Paul's: it resonated with the general appeal Judaism held for Gentiles in the ancient world, and it presented a coherent position on Christ's relationship to Judaism.

### The General Appeal of Judaism for Gentiles

There was in the Hellenistic world, just as today, an attractiveness to the Jewish way of life. Tacitus's description of the Jews gives a picture of how they appeared to a pagan. He comments that "the Jews are extremely loyal toward one another, and always ready to show compassion, but toward every other people they feel only hate and enmity. They sit apart at meals and they sleep apart . . . they adopt circumcision to distinguish themselves from other peoples by this difference."[1] The Jews' tight-knit and separate society was repulsive to some outsiders,[2] yet there also seems to be a grudging respect for its quality of communal life.

The central, all-encompassing nature of the Jewish law offered both protection and moral guidance. In a social world in which the rule of law often appeared arbitrary, a community that defined itself by its legal framework would have been especially attractive. In the first-century Mediterranean world, the ethical life was a topic of discussion, as witnessed by the various philosophical schools of the time, and Judaism was a compelling option for the morally serious. Furthermore, the ancient heritage of the Jewish faith held an allure to the ancients, who revered the traditional.[3] The antiquity of the Torah was one of its chief recommendations; Josephus writes about Moses: "our legislator is the most ancient of all legislators in the records of the whole world."[4]

There appear to have been a significant number of pagans who associated themselves with the synagogues. From ancient Jewish inscriptions, particularly those discovered recently at Aphrodisias, it is clear that some Gentiles, termed "god-fearers" *(theosebeis)*, attached themselves to synagogues even though they did not wholly adopt a Jewish lifestyle.[5] Juvenal gives a particularly interesting description of the "problem" of these god-fearers in Rome.

> Some who have had a father who reveres the Sabbath, worship nothing but the clouds, and the divinity of the heavens, and see no difference between eating swine's flesh, from which their father abstained, and that of man; and in time they take to circumcision. Having been wont to flout the laws of Rome, they learn and practise and revere the Jewish law, and all that Moses handed down in his secret tome, forbidding to point out the way to any not worshipping the same rites, and conducting none but the circumcised to the desired fountain. For all which the father was to blame, who gave up every seventh day to idleness, keeping it apart from all the concerns of life.[6]

Part of the reason that the contending evangelists were able to engage the Galatians' attention was that the Galatians wanted to be attached to an ancient religion. It is evident that they were concerned about inheriting the promises to Abraham. Furthermore, it is clear that the Galatians desired moral guidance. Paul's repeated claim that faith makes one righteous and that the Spirit aids in the process of becoming righteous (5:5) is a response to a situation in which there was a desire for moral instruction.

Given that other ancient Gentiles respected and even adopted the Jewish lifestyle, the attraction to Judaism exhibited by Paul's Galatian converts should not be seen as a gullible or wayward attitude. The Galatians, like many other Gentiles, may have regarded the Jewish way of life as a particularly attractive opportunity for belonging to a respectable ancient religion that provided moral guidance.[7] Paul's gospel seems to have appeared less than satisfactory to them in comparison with the rival evangelists' presentation of a Torah-observant gospel.

### The Rival Evangelists' Gospel Appeared More Logical Than Paul's

The second main advantage that the other gospel had was that it made logical sense. Paul's rivals could argue that since Christ was the Messiah expected by Judaism, those who believed in him should observe the Jewish law, which entailed circumcision (Gen. 17:10–14).

In response to this alternate gospel Paul is at pains to present his unique understanding of the relationship between Christ and Judaism, and so between Gentiles and Jews. Paul agrees with his opponents that believers in Christ inherit the promises of God to Israel, but he does not think that this inheritance requires them to follow Jewish practice. Gentile believers receive the blessing of Abraham in the form of the Spirit rather than through covenant observance (3:29–4:7). Christ is not the Messiah expected by Judaism, but is the crucified one (2:19–3:1; 5:11; 6:14) whose scandalous and unprecedented death has changed everything for those who believe in him. Believers are in a new creation (6:15), dead to the law (2:19) and the flesh (5:24). Christ fulfills God's promise of righteousness for Gentiles (3:8) in a way unanticipated by Jews. In effect, for Paul the gospel is not logically coherent, for it does not follow directly from Jewish hopes and beliefs. This is why Paul makes the point that he received the gospel through revelation (1:12).

### Paul's Opponents in Galatia

Paul may have expected that his letter would be heard by the rival evangelists as well as by the Galatian believers. These evangelists were preaching a version of the faith that was very different from Paul's and Paul views them as enemies on several levels. They are enemies of the truth of the gospel (1:7–9; 3:1; 6:12). Consequently, they are also enemies of the spiritual well-being of the Galatians (5:2–4). Finally, they are enemies of the Galatians' loyalty to Paul, their father in the faith (5:10; cf. 4:19, where Paul calls the Galatians his "dear children"). These levels are interconnected for Paul because he identifies himself completely with the truth of the gospel (1:8; 1:12; 1:19–21; 4:16) and sees himself as the one who knows what is right for the Galatians and the one in whom they should trust (4:12; 5:2; 5:10–12).

The letter gives several strong clues concerning the nature of the gospel preached by the rival evangelists. We know that it was different from the gospel that Paul preached (1:6). A brief summary of what Paul asserts about his gospel provides some indication of the nature of the opposing gospel.

Paul says that his gospel is for Gentiles (1:16; 2:2; 2:9). Gentiles are not required to become Jewish proselytes; they can remain as Gentiles (2:14), for justification comes through faith in Jesus Christ alone (2:16). The death of Christ is central to Paul's message; he says that he glories in nothing except the cross of Christ (6:14), and he summarizes his preaching to the Galatians as a public portrayal of Christ crucified (3:1). The death of Christ delivers believers from the present evil age (1:4), in which humans are caught because of sin (1:4). By believing in the efficacy of the death of Christ, believers are crucified with Christ and so die to the law (2:19–20), for Christ's death redeemed believers from the curse of the law (3:13). Believers also die to the flesh (5:24) and so become righteous through the promised Spirit (3:14; 5:5). The cross is central to Paul's gospel and is directly and inextricably linked to righteousness by faith. The option of becoming righteous exists because of Christ's death (2:21). There is little evidence from the letter to the Galatians that Paul stressed Christ's resurrection, although the resurrection is presupposed in his concept of believers being "in Christ" (e.g., 3:14, 26; 5:6).

The intruding evangelists preached a gospel that must have been almost diametrically opposed to Paul's in at least two ways. First, they were advocating that Gentile believers adopt Jewish practice. These evangelists presented Torah-observance so attractively that the Galatian men were seriously considering circumcision, a step that would unequivocally identify the Galatians with the Jewish nation and a law-observant lifestyle. In the ancient world circumcision was a clear sign of being a Jew (even though it was was practiced by some pagan people such as the Egyptians). Jews were often described as "the circumcised," and Justin Martyr has the Jew Trypho call himself a "Hebrew of the circumcision."[8]

The intruding evangelists were messianic Jews who considered following the Jewish law essential for a believer in Jesus Christ. Although not all Jewish Christians took this view, as the Jewish Christians Paul and Peter demonstrate, Acts provides corroborative evidence that some did. Luke writes that "some of the believers who belonged to the party of the Pharisees [believed that] 'The Gentiles must be circumcised and required to obey the law of Moses' " (15:5).

The second way that the gospel of the intruding evangelists differed from that of Paul was that it either deemphasized the death of Christ or understood Christ's death differently. In Galatians, Paul places a strong emphasis on the death of Christ and makes a direct connection between Christ's death and righteousness by faith (e.g., 2:21). The gospel of his rivals may have had some similarities at this point to the Jewish Christian gospel presented in 1 Peter (3:18–4:2), which does not draw a direct connection between Christ's death and righteousness by faith. For Paul, a gospel that includes law observance (at least a certain type of law observance) is a gospel in which "the offense of the cross has been abolished" (5:11).[9] Presumably Paul describes the cross as an offense because it contradicts all previous Jewish understandings of how righteousness should be attained. For the rival evangelists, it appears that the cross and righteousness by faith are not closely connected. For the apostle, the cross and righteousness by faith are one and the same thing.

While a few scholars have suggested that the intruding evangelists were Gentiles who had themselves accepted circumcision,[10] the most straightforward explanation is that the opponents were believers in Christ who were Jews. For them faith in Jesus fulfilled Jewish hopes but did not redefine Judaism. Consequently, to the rival evangelists it was unthinkable to discontinue a Jewish lifestyle after belief in Jesus. Apocryphal writings from the first two centuries of Christianity such as the *Epistle of Peter to James* and the *Testimony Regarding the Recipients of the Epistle,* give evidence for such a viewpoint. In these texts "lawless" Christianity is considered heretical[11] and leadership in the community is open only to "a man who as one who has been circumcised is a believing Christian."[12]

The question arises as to whether or not the intruding missionaries were preaching under the authority of the Jerusalem church.[13] Paul is at pains to clarify for the Galatians the independence of his gospel as regards Jerusalem and that the acknowledged leaders in Jerusalem recognized the validity of his mission to Gentiles (2:9) and these facts indicate that Jerusalem was a factor in the rival evangelists' platform. They likely censured Paul's gospel by claiming that the authority of Jerusalem was not behind Paul but behind them. Paul responds to this claim by asserting that the acknowledged leaders in Jerusalem accepted his gospel (2:7–9). From Paul's account in 2:1–10 it appears that there was division in the Jerusalem church, but he asserts that the significant leaders accepted his understanding of the manner in which Gentiles could be included in the faith. While we cannot attain certainty as to whether the intruding evangelists were backed by Jerusalem, the most likely hypothesis is that they were acting under the authority of part of the Jerusalem church, and that another part of the church was on Paul's side.[14]

When Paul writes this letter he probably expects his audience to include his opponents, who are now a significant factor in the Galatian churches. By addressing the logic of the alternate gospel—that to believe in the Jewish Messiah was to become a Jew—Paul seeks to undermine their current influence and preempt counterarguments that could result from the public reading of his letter. In effect Paul gives those still loyal to him in Galatia intellectual ammunition with which to fight the proponents of the alternate gospel.[15]

It is understandable why Christian Jews would want to persuade Christian Gentiles to adopt the Jewish way of life. Both theological and social factors were likely at play. For Christian Jews, Jesus was the Messiah and belief in him meant inheriting the promises to Israel. It seemed only right, then, for all Christians to act like Jews. Furthermore, it would have been difficult for Christian Jews to be part of this new group within Judaism. Close social interaction with Gentile Christians would have made their position in the Jewish community increasingly awkward. For the sake of their own consciences and so as to maintain their standing in the Jewish community, it is easy to understand why Christian Jews might have encouraged Christian Gentiles to adopt Jewish practice.

This commentary will refer to Paul's opponents either as confusers (cf. 1:7; 5:10), agitators (cf. 5:12), troublemakers, rival or intruding evangelists, or the circumcisers (cf. 6:12).

## Audience and Date

As will be explained below, this commentary will not use Acts in determining the audience of the letter. This is not because the information in Acts is considered historically unreliable but because of the notorious difficulty in squaring any chronological information that Galatians gives us with information in Acts. Yet, many have thought it possible to harmonize the data in Acts with that in Galatians. When such a project is undertaken, the questions "Who were the Galatians?" and "When was the letter written?" become necessarily interrelated.[16]

Answering the first of these questions is problematic, because Acts refers to two areas within the Roman province of Galatia in which Paul journeyed and worked. In Acts 13 and 14 Luke writes that Paul visited Pamphylia and Pisidia (13:13–14) and preached in Iconium (14:1), Lystra, Derbe (14:6), and Antioch (14:21). These locations were in the southern part of the province of Galatia. Acts also refers to Paul journeying through the "region of Phrygia and Galatia" (16:6; 18:23), that is, to the northern part of the territory.

If the letter is addressed to churches in the south, then, according to the account in Acts, Galatians could be written relatively early in Paul's missionary work. Following Luke's chronology it is conceivable that Galatians was written prior to the Apostolic Council (Acts 15:1–29). If the letter were written to churches in the northern part of the region, however, then according to Acts it was written after the Apostolic Council and most probably somewhat later in Paul's missionary endeavors.

The issue of audience is usually decided on the basis of more than geography alone. For instance, those who take the position that Paul wrote to a south Galatian destination might do so because they think that an early date is the best explanation of why Paul, writing to a church in which his law-free gospel is being attacked by people with close ties to Jerusalem, does not bolster his case by reference to the Council. Paul does not mention the Council because it has not yet occurred. Another argument employed in favor of the south Galatian hypothesis is that Peter's action at Antioch, as recounted by Paul in Galatians 2:11–14, is more understandable before the Council than after.[17]

Those who argue in favor of the north Galatian position interpret the phrase "I first preached the gospel to you" (4:13) to mean that Paul has made a subsequent visit to the region. According to these scholars, Paul's first visit is that referred to in Acts 16:6 and the second in Acts 18:23. A case for a north Galatian destination is built also on the observation that since the letter is addressed to Gentiles it cannot have been addressed to Iconium, Lystra, and Derbe, which had sizeable Jewish populations.[18]

By and large scholars adopt the north Galatian hypothesis, perhaps in large measure because it typically places the letter later in Paul's life.[19] A later date has two main advantages. First, it allows the Jerusalem visit of Galatians 2 to be identified with the Jerusalem Council of Acts 15. Even though this creates the problem of why Paul does not use the Council's decision in his letter, it does allow the wonderful convenience of two independent accounts of the same visit. Second, a later date may explain similarities in theme between Galatians and Romans.[20]

Yet a decision about a north or south Galatian destination, that is, a decision based on trying to square the information in Acts with that in Galatians, does not answer the puzzle of the date of the letter. It is possible that the letter is addressed to churches from Paul's earliest journey, yet written later in his career; and it is also possible that it is composed soon after Paul's second journey, making the letter one of his earliest.[21]

The questions "Who were the Galatians?" and "When was the letter written?" have also been debated apart from the information in Acts. Some argue that since Acts is both a secondhand account and one with its own agenda,[22] the best course of action is to work with the letter to the Galatians alone. So several recent studies have largely ignored the evidence of Acts.[23]

The position of this commentary is that the issue of the destination and date of Galatians is exegetically important primarily as it relates to the question of whether or not the letter is written after a meeting such as Luke records in Acts 15. That is, the most significant factor in answering the questions of who the Galatians were and when the letter was written is whether or not to use the information of the Jerusalem Council (Acts 15:1–29) when interpreting Paul's meeting with the church leaders in Jerusalem, described in Galatians 2:1–10. It seems that the only way to decide this is to compare Paul's reference to this meeting in Jerusalem with Luke's record of the Council.[24]

### The Council at Jerusalem in Acts 15:1–29 Compared with the Meeting Recorded in Galatians 2:1–10

There are several similarities between the events described in Acts 15:1–29 and Galatians 2:1–10. Both involve trips to Jerusalem in which Barnabas accompanies Paul. In Acts, Luke writes that they were also accompanied by "some other believers" (15:2), and Galatians refers to Titus, who could have been among this group. In Acts and Galatians, the law-free gospel is challenged by believers who were somewhat separate from the central leadership. In both accounts the most pivotal believers accept Paul's group and gospel. Peter plays a central role in each presentation of the meeting, and the outcome in both is agreement that Paul's gospel to the Gentiles is from God.

There are, however, some significant differences between the accounts in Acts 15 and Galatians 2. In Acts, the challenge raised at the meeting by Pharisaic believers is presented as directly related to the matter upon which Paul, Barnabas, and company have journeyed to Jerusalem, namely, whether or not it is necessary for Gentiles to be circumcised and keep the law of Moses. The ensuing hearing focuses on the matter raised by these Pharisaic believers. In Galatians, however, Paul recounts a meeting much less influenced by those he calls the "false brothers." In Paul's account their view is not taken seriously by the acknowledged leaders. Furthermore, Paul's own story conveys the impression that the leaders were simply convinced by what they saw of Paul's gospel.

Some of the differences between Luke's record in Acts and Paul's in Galatians may be differences of perspective. For example, Paul would want to convey the impression that he had a significant degree of control over the proceedings as well as to discount the validity of the alternate viewpoint. Luke's concern to highlight the control of the Jerusalem leadership may have led him to present a more "top-down" portrayal of the event. Another variation that could be one of perspective is the difference in the final decisions reached at the meeting. In Paul's account the agreement reached at the meeting concerns the division of labor and responsibilities: Peter has a mission to the circumcised and Paul to the uncircumcised (Gal. 2:7–9). In Paul's record the debate focuses on the consequences of a Torah-free gospel for mission. In Acts, however, there is no decision to divide the evangelistic field. The point of the council is to debate whether Gentiles as Gentiles could be part of the church.

Another difference that might reflect varying standpoints and agendas is that in Acts Peter turns the tide by reminding his hearers that "some time ago" God had determined he should go among the Gentiles (15:7), whereas in Galatians Paul says that the acknowledged leaders recognized that Peter "had been given the task of preaching the gospel to the Jews," and he calls Peter "an apostle to the Jews" (2:7–8). In Acts the force of Peter's argument rests on his own experience of and commitment to the Gentile mission, whereas in Galatians Peter makes the difference at the Jerusalem meeting because he is so clearly identified with a mission to the Jews.

While differences in the accounts such as those above might be explained as due to the particular perspectives and purposes in writing of Paul and Luke, there are also differences of fact. One such difference concerns the relative time of Paul's conflict at Antioch. In Acts Paul goes up to Jerusalem because of a conflict at Antioch, but in Galatians (2:11–14) Paul does not describe a confrontation at Antioch until after he has told the story of his visit to Jerusalem. Paul does not state that the incident at Antioch prompted his Jerusalem trip. Rather, Paul says that he went up because of revelation. Furthermore, there are reasons to doubt that the episode at Antioch recorded in Acts 15:1–2 is the same as that recounted in Galatians 2:11–14. In Galatians Peter is present at the Antioch incident, but Acts does not report this; in fact, it presents Peter as able to mediate the debate that arose as a result.[25]

Another notable difference between Acts 15 and Galatians 2 is the result of the agreement of the Jerusalem Council. In Acts this is a decision that, while Gentiles are acceptable in the church, they are constrained by the command "to abstain from food polluted by idols, from sexual immorality, from the meat of strangled animals and from blood" (15:20).[26] This directive is to be conveyed to the church at Antioch in the form of a letter sent with Paul and Barnabas, who are accompanied on their return journey by some of the Jerusalem church leaders. In Galatians, on the other hand, there is no reference to such a command (or to Jerusalem Christians returning with Paul to Antioch). It is decided that Paul does have a mission to the Gentiles and that it should be exercised without restraint from those whose mission is to the Jews. In Galatians the acknowledged leaders require only that Paul and Barnabas "should continue to remember the poor" (2:10).[27]

If Galatians 2 and Acts 15 are describing the same event, the only way to explain these differences of fact would be to surmise that Paul or Luke have changed facts to suit their purposes. But taking this position leads us into the realm of speculation, in which any piece of evidence can take on chameleon-like quality.

Thus, given that the Jerusalem visit of Acts 15 is so different from the one Paul describes in Galatians 2,[28] the most cautious approach is to regard the two accounts as referring to two separate events. The limit of our knowledge in this regard is that, when Paul wrote Galatians, he had been to a meeting in Jerusalem in which he felt his legitimate authority to exercise a Gentile mission had been recognized.[29]

### Galatians Is One of Paul's Earlier Letters

The best alternative to using Acts to date Galatians is to determine where it fits among the sequence of Paul's letters. Some have proposed that the relative chronological order of the letters may be determined by tracing development in Paul's theological thinking, particularly his thinking about eschatology.[30] Such proposals necessarily rely on assumptions about how Paul's thinking might have developed and often do not adequately take into account the fact that his letters are not primarily witnesses to a developing theological mind but are the apostle's responses to distinctive circumstances. Differences in Paul's statements on issues such as eschatology, the law, or justification are largely attributable to the differences in the situations he is addressing. Therefore it is problematic to trace the development of these ideas. And, as Knox has outlined, using theology to determine the order of Paul's letters has produced a wide variety of chronological schemes.[31]

However, one piece of evidence does allow us to trace something of the relative order of the letters: the collection project for the poor saints in Jerusalem.[32] Tracing the evidence backwards, we find that in Romans Paul is in the final stage of the collection project. He tells his Roman readers that he is on his way to Jerusalem with money that had been contributed by the Gentiles of Macedonia and Achaia (Rom. 15:25–27). In the course of encouraging the Corinthian church, which is situated in Achaia, to give liberally to the collection project, Paul tells them that the churches of Macedonia have given generously (2 Cor. 8:1–2; 9:4). In 1 Corinthians 16:1 he mentions the collection project to the Corinthians. Macedonia is not mentioned as part of the project, since he is on his way there as he writes (16:5), but Galatia is mentioned. On the assumption that Paul would have mentioned the churches of Galatia in 2 Corinthians and Romans if they had still been participants in the project, it appears that at some point between the writing of 1 and 2 Corinthians the Galatian churches dropped out of Paul's collection project.[33]

The question now becomes whether or not the letter to the Galatians was written when the Galatian churches were still involved in the project. While the letter witnesses to mounting tension between Paul and the Galatians, Paul clearly has a relationship with them and furthermore feels free to mention the collection project (2:10). This suggests that at the time of writing the churches of Galatia were involved in the collection.

Tracing references to the collection project cannot tell us whether or not the letter was written prior to 1 Corinthians, but the fact that Galatia is not mentioned as involved in the collection in 2 Corinthians 8–9 strongly suggests that the letter was written prior to 2 Corinthians.[34] If this interpretation of the evidence is correct, it would make Galatians one of Paul's earlier writings.

The letter does not indicate the place from which it was sent. That there are such numerous and varying proposals (e.g., Ephesus, Macedonia, and Corinth) indicates the difficulty scholars have had coming to a conclusive decision. Fortunately for us, no exegetical significance is attached to determining the place of composition.

### The Galatian Churches Were Probably in Southern Galatia

It would help our historical imagination if we knew whether the letter was addressed to churches in the north or south of the Galatian province, since each region had a different cultural character. The Roman province of Galatia was in central Asia Minor (modern Turkey), extending in the north from the Black Sea to the Mediterranean in the south. The Roman presence was strong in the south, where Roman legions were garrisoned, and in the early part of the first century A.D. Roman roads connected the important Roman establishments of southern Galatia.

In the north the Roman presence was not so strongly felt. Roman roads were not built in the north until the 70s, and the Celtic tribes that had formed the basis of the kingdom of Amyntas, which the Romans annexed to form the province of Galatia (25 B.C.), were less affected by Roman culture.

The natives of Galatia were called both Galatians and Celts, for a group of Celts that originated in central Europe had come to Asia Minor searching for new land in the early third century B.C. Strabo says that the three tribes that came to "Galatae" "wandered about for a long time, and after they had overrun the country that was subject to the Attalic and the Bithynian kings . . . they received the present Galatia, or Gallo-Graecia, as it is called."[35] Eventually this Pontic heartland in which the Celts had settled was made into a Roman province.

The Celts, or Galatians, were known for customs thought barbaric by the Greeks and Romans. The historian S. Mitchell writes:

> The Galatians lived on the margin of civilized life, plundering temples, sacking cities, and inspiring fear, well-merited, among the defenseless population of the Asian countryside. The damage they caused far outweighed the contribution they provided: an unceasing supply of mercenary soldiers; and a series of assassins responsible for the murder of several Hellenistic kings.[36]

Athenaeus records that around 90 B.C. Posidonius made this observation about Celts in Gaul:

> The Celts sometimes have gladiatorial contests during dinner. Having assembled under arms, they indulge in sham fights and practise feints with one another; sometimes they proceed even to the point of wounding each other, and then, exasperated by this, if the company does not intervene, they go so far as to kill.[37]

Viewed by the Greeks and Romans as "the archetypal barbarians,"[38] the Galatians were "considered to be large, unpredictable simpletons, ferocious and highly dangerous when angry, but without stamina and easy to trick."[39]

Unfortunately, it is not possible to be certain which region of the Galatian province the recipients of Paul's letter lived in. We may, however, note three factors in favor of the southern region. First, the letter is addressed to people fluent in Greek. Although some have suggested that the Hellenized Celtic cities of the north, such as Ankyra and Pessinus, may be a likely designation,[40] the Greek language was most probably more common in the south, making a southern destination for Galatians more likely.[41]

The second factor making a southern Galatian destination more probable than a northern one is that at the time of Paul's missionizing the Roman roads were in the south. This would make the south by far the more convenient region for Paul's efforts.[42] The third factor favoring a south Galatian address is that there is no evidence for Jews in the north.[43] Paul's letter, however, is a response to the influence of Jewish Christian missionizing. That the Galatians were open to adopting Jewish practice strongly suggests that they knew something about Judaism prior to the arrival of the rival evangelists. It is hard to imagine how Galatian pagans who had converted to Paul's law-free gospel would be open to such a message and lifestyle or would see how it fit with their new faith unless they had some previous experience with Judaism.[44]

Some have used Paul's epithet "foolish Galatians" (3:1) to argue that the letter was addressed to the northern Gauls. Yet, as Mitchell points out, it could just as well be that while this derogatory designation may seem out of place applied to the southern Galatian city dwellers, "it is part of Paul's reproach that he equates them with the barbarous people who had given their name to the province, and who themselves had a quite independent reputation for simple-mindedness."[45]

## The Author Paul

Modern interpretation of Galatians is affected by whether or not the reader of the letter conceives of Paul as speaking from within Judaism. If we think of Paul as remaining within Judaism, then it is legitimate to use Jewish categories and expectations in interpreting his writings. If we determine that after his conversion Paul did not consider himself part of Judaism, then we must approach his Christology and scriptural interpretation from a different framework.

Undoubtedly Paul remained an ethnic Jew all his life; during the period in which Paul lived Jews regarded themselves as Jewish by virtue of being born of a Jewish mother.[46] But Jews connected their ethnicity also with religious practice and belief, and there was a lively debate about which form of the Jewish religion was correct. The various forms of Judaism in the first century, from that evidenced at Qumran, to Pharisaic, to Sadducean, to philosophical (Philo) all witness to the diverse ways that Jews interpreted the religious aspect of their identity. Although Paul remained a Jew in the ethnic sense, the question is, did he think that his faith in Christ was another form of Judaism?

### Did Paul Remain a Religious Jew?

Many scholars maintain that Paul remained an ethnic as well as a religious Jew after faith in Christ. Those who take this view diverge over the way Paul's faith in Jesus as Messiah functions within the framework of his gospel. W. D. Davies writes that, "throughout his life Paul was a practicing Jew who never ceased to insist that his gospel was first to the Jews, who also expected Jewish Christians to persist in their loyalty to the Torah of Judaism."[47] For Davies, Paul is "a Pharisee who accepted Jesus of Nazareth, crucified and raised from the dead, as the Messiah. . . . In Paul's response to Christ, the Messiah, he came to understand the Christian life as patterned after that of Judaism."[48]

Some others who regard Paul as remaining within Judaism after he came to faith in Christ place less stress on Paul's belief in Jesus as the Jewish Messiah, while maintaining that Paul regarded Christ as the fulfillment of Israel's hopes. J. C. Beker writes that "Paul was and remained a Jew. . . . For Paul, Christianity is not a *nova religio* but the answer to Israel's longing for the messianic age."[49] Beker's apocalyptic and theocentric interpretation of Paul focuses attention away from Jesus as the Messiah and toward his role in initiating and guaranteeing the age of God's visibly triumphant reign. For Beker, Paul understood that the Messiah had come, although without his kingdom. He writes: "Christ is not so much the fulfillment of God's promises as the guarantee or confirmation of these promises."[50]

Knox regards Paul as continuing to think of himself as a Jew, but because he believes that Jesus was the Messiah, a Jew who was "a member of a new people—new because it has a new 'spirit' and is open to all of every nation simply on the condition of faith, and yet old since it is Israel become itself, the fulfillment of God's ancient promises."[51] For A. Segal, Paul is a first-century Jewish apocalypticist[52] who leaves behind Pharisaic Judaism by joining a Gentile Christian community[53] and as such is "a convert from one Jewish sect to another."[54] In Segal's view, Paul converted to a "heretical form of Judaism."[55]

### Did Paul Break with Judaism?

The alternate view is that Paul's faith did not fit within Judaism. E. P. Sanders considers that after the revelation of God's Son, Paul, while not perceiving "that his gospel and his missionary activity impl[ied] a break with Judaism,"[56] nevertheless through his belief and practice effects such a break. What Paul's faith entails is the creation of a "third entity." As Sanders puts it:

> Paul . . . thought of the church as the fulfillment of the promises to Abraham. In that sense it was not at all a new religion. Jews who entered the Christian movement did not have to convert in the way Gentiles did: they did not have to renounce their god, nor, at least in theory, observance of the law. It was not established by admitting Gentiles to Israel according to the flesh . . . but by admitting all, whether Jew or Greek, into the body of Christ by faith in him.[57]

In Sanders's words, Paul's religion is "basically different from anything known from Palestinian Judaism."[58] Paul "simply saw the old dispensation as worthless in comparison with the new. . . . In short, this is what Paul finds wrong in Judaism: it is not Christianity."[59] S. Mason takes Galatians as Paul's "fullest statement on Judaism to his Gentile churches" and determines that in it Paul demonstrates that he "no longer identifies himself with the Jewish people."[60]

### This Commentary's Position—Somewhere In Between

The vast problem of Paul's relationship to Judaism cannot be fully discussed here. It is, however, important to outline the approach taken in this commentary, which fits somewhere between those who see Paul as a messianic Jew and those who consider that he separated himself from Judaism.

To find a position that might explain all of the evidence requires a less than tidy solution. There are ways in which Paul remains connected to Judaism. Paul writes that Christ was born under the law (Gal. 4:4), that God's action in Christ was for the Jews (4:5), that faith in Christ allowed Gentiles to inherit the promises to Abraham (3:9, 14), and that the circumcised belong in the faith also (2:9). Even though Christ's death abolished the law (2:21), the law may be fulfilled through love (5:14), of which believers are especially capable (5:13). Furthermore, there are places where he seems to stress the continuity between his gospel and that of the first Jewish believers and their Jewish hopes. For instance, in 1 Corinthians 15 Paul writes that his gospel is one that came through revelation and teaching. What he received and accepted from those who were believers before him, he says, is that Christ died "according to the Scriptures" (1 Cor. 15:3). Paul maintains that the gospel he preaches emerged from Judaism, fulfills the promises of Judaism, and is for Jews.

However, there are indications that Paul thought of his faith as novel. He claims that his faith came through revelation and that he was not taught it (1:12). Paul's stress on his gospel as being about the crucified Christ and his recognition that this is a scandal to those who adhere to Jewish ways (5:11) demonstrate his appreciation of how unexpected his own faith was within Judaism. It must have been clear to Paul that a gospel to Gentiles that did not require them to adopt the Torah was at odds with Jewish expectations for the fulfillment of God's promises to Israel. This gospel did not fit with any established pattern but rather inaugurated a new creation into which the existing interpretation of Judaism did not fit (Gal. 6:15). Even Paul's apocalyptic bent[61] does not fit standard Jewish apocalyptic, for there is little in Jewish apocalyptic that anticipates either a crucified messiah or a faith that speaks of being incorporated into another being ("in Christ").[62]

Further, while there may be many circumstantial reasons to explain why Paul says the negative things he does about Judaism (see esp. 1 Thess. 2:15–16; Phil. 3:7–9; 2 Cor. 3:7–10), the fact that he says them suggests that at some level Paul regards his gospel as separate from Judaism, or at least as separate from Judaism that has not recognized Christ.

Neither the view that regards Paul as seeing faith in Christ as the fulfillment of Jewish messianic expectations nor the view that regards him as separating himself from Judaism accounts for all the evidence. Paul thinks of the gospel as a new thing with consequences for Judaism. In other words, while Paul regards his gospel as new and unexpected, he at the same time considers it a message born out of Judaism that can speak to Judaism. While it will not fit within contemporary Judaism, the gospel is nevertheless an invitation to Jews. Paul's gospel affirms God's faithfulness to the Jews throughout history (3:21–25) but requires Jews and Gentiles to see that a new thing has happened that now affects the way Judaism is to understand itself. Paul, therefore, understands his gospel as new and separate from existing Judaism, yet as also having consequences for Jewish self-understanding.[63]

This complicated relationship witnesses to the commonplace experience of a person's separation from the people, traditions, or worldviews of his or her past. One example of such separation is when a teenager grows up and comes to define herself independently from her parents. Part of separation is defining herself over against her parents. The teenager seeks to redefine the relationship she has with her parents. Once she discovers herself she then can invite her parents to participate in her life, on her terms. This same dynamic may be at work for Paul, who after the revelation stands apart from Judaism while still remaining in some sense connected to it. Paul wants Jews to participate in his gospel, on the terms that he sets.

And so Paul has a complex relationship with Judaism. He knows himself to be an ethnic Jew, but he is not a practicing Jew (Gal. 2:15–16). He is a Jew to whom something new has been revealed, a Jew with a mission to the Gentiles, but nevertheless a Jew who sees his message as affecting Judaism. Paul stands apart from Judaism and can speak of it as something other (1:14). And yet he considers what he preaches to be in line with the promises of God to Israel. Paul knows that his message, with the crucified Christ at its core, is unanticipated, scandalous, and even offensive (5:11) to Jews. This goes a long way toward explaining why Paul stresses the crucified Christ. This revelation entailed the creation of a new community, a community in which Jews and Gentiles live together on the basis of faith in the crucified Christ. Jews are now invited to see their faith in a whole new light, to consider that neither circumcision nor uncircumcision counted for anything. Paul understood the revelation to have consequences for the religion out of which it came.

Taking such a view of Paul's relationship to Judaism affects in several ways the exegesis of Galatians. First, we may not expect Paul's interpretation of Scripture to be in line with any typical Jewish interpretation. Subsequent to his call, Paul's reading of Scripture is based on the self-understanding that to him has been revealed something entirely new. We should not expect his exegesis to correspond to existing traditions, and we may expect it to be idiosyncratic. Second, we will not presume that Paul invested the term "Christ" with first-century messianic expectations. This interpretive stance makes room for the evidence that Paul does not feel constrained to explain the glaring problem of how the crucified and risen Jesus could be a messiah, when that so obviously contradicted Jewish expectations. Though Paul considered Jesus to be the Jewish Messiah, he argues not that Jewish *messianic* expectations were fulfilled in Jesus but rather that God's fundamental promise that Israel would be a blessing to the nations is fulfilled in Jesus. When Paul uses the term "Christ" messianically he redefines its messianic connotations (e.g., Gal. 3:16).[64]

Chiefly Paul uses the designation "Christ" as a proper name rather than investing it with messianic meaning.[65] The corpus of Paul's letters witnesses to the fact that when Paul speaks to Gentiles about Jesus Christ he speaks of Christ's universal lordship, not of his Jewish messiahship.[66]

One of Paul's more lucid statements on the matter of the relationship of his gospel to Judaism is found in Romans: "but now the righteousness of God has been manifested apart from law, although the law and the prophets bear witness to it" (Rom. 3:21, RSV).

## Paul's Gospel

This commentary accepts the view that justification by faith, while an extremely important concept in Paul, is not his most comprehensive description of the gospel. The defining shape of Paul's gospel is what A. Schweitzer calls "the experience of union with Christ"[67] and what E. P. Sanders terms "participationist eschatology."[68]

Paul characterizes the gospel as being about the crucified and risen Son of God (e.g., Rom. 1:4; 1 Cor. 1:17), in whose death and resurrection believers now participate (e.g., Rom. 6:2–11; 2 Cor. 1:5; 5:14–15; Phil. 2:5–11; 3:10–11), to whom believers now belong (e.g., Rom. 7:4; 1 Cor. 3:23; 6:19; Phil. 3:12), in whom believers are (e.g., Rom. 8:1; 1 Cor. 6:15; 12:13; 15:58; 2 Cor. 1:21; Phil. 3:9; 4:7), who is in believers (e.g., Rom. 8:10; 2 Cor. 13:5), and whose death and resurrection allow believers to hope in the future (e.g., Rom. 5:2, 9; 6:5; 8:18–24; 1 Cor. 1:7–9; 11:26; 15:20; 2 Cor. 4:14; Phil. 1:10; 3:20–21; 1 Thess. 1:10; 4:13–18; 5:9–11; 2 Thess. 1:7–10). Perhaps the most succinct way that Paul describes his gospel is either the statement in Romans that God predestined believers "to be conformed to the likeness of his Son" (8:29; cf. 1 Cor. 15:49; 2 Cor. 3:18; 2 Thess. 2:14) or the statement in 2 Corinthians: "if any one is in Christ, he is a new creation" (5:17).

This understanding of Paul's gospel will lend a certain nuance to this commentary's interpretation of Galatians. For, while the letter contains the famous statement that "a man is not justified by observing the law, . . . because by observing the law no one will be justified" (2:16), this will be interpreted in the context of a gospel shaped by the idea that "a man" is incorporated into Christ's death and resurrection and becomes a new creation. Recognition of the scope and uniqueness of Paul's gospel requires that when reading Galatians we intermingle the concept of justification by faith with the concepts of dying and living with Christ the Son of God (2:20), being in Christ (3:26–27), having Christ in believers (4:19) and belonging to Christ (3:29; 5:24). The doctrine of justification by faith is not Paul's gospel in a nutshell, but it is part of the complex of his gospel.

This brings us directly to the issue of the meaning of the phrase *pistis Christou*, "faith in Christ Jesus," since this central Pauline phrase takes on a particular shading depending on what shape Paul's gospel is considered to have. The phrase occurs at Galatians 2:16 and also at Galatians 3:22 (see also Rom. 3:22, 26; Eph. 3:12; Phil. 3:9). The options for translation of the Greek *pistis Christou* are either faith *in* Christ Jesus (an objective genitive) or faith *of* Christ Jesus (a subjective genitive). In recent years a strong argument has been raised in favor of the second option.[69] This commentary adopts the subjective genitive reading "faith of Christ," or "Christ's faith." The significance of such a decision is that in a verse such as 2:16, where the phrase *pistis Christou* occurs twice, the translation becomes: "we know that a person is justified not by the works of law but through Christ's faith *(pistis Christou)*. And we have come to have faith in Christ Jesus, so that we might be justified by Christ's faith *(pistis Christou)* and not by doing the works of law."

My reasons for this choice do not include that advanced by A. G. Hebert[70] and T. Torrance,[71] that the Hebrew idea of faithfulness underlies Paul's term *pistis*. I am convinced by J. Barr that their proposed grammatical evidence has wrongly confused theological and linguistic argumentation[72] and presumed that a Greek word could be "dominated by a Hebrew concept."[73] Neither do my reasons include the fact that the subjective genitive translation clears up the redundancies in a verse like Gal. 2:16 (when the phrase *pistis Christou* is translated subjectively the threefold repetition of "faith in Christ" is eliminated). Repetition was an honored rhetorical strategy. Moreover, I do not think that the issue can be decided at the level of grammar. There are valid grammatical reasons for choosing either the objective or subjective reading.[74]

My reason for choosing the subjective genitive translation of *pistis Christou* is that such a translation here (as well as at Gal. 3:33; Phil. 3:9; Rom. 3:22, 26) brings these verses in line with the central message of Paul—that believers are "in Christ." A subjective genitive translation properly lessens (while not obliterating) the focus on the act of human faith and consequently on the doctrine of justification by faith. Furthermore, a subjective genitive translation provides an appropriate parallel between Jesus' faith and that of Abraham (3:6–9). As noted by I. G. Wallis, a proponent of the "of Christ" reading, Jesus' faith is:

> not only the context for God's offer of renewed relationship, but also the context for response to that offer: people may believe because their faith is a function of being found in Christ and so of being a part of Christ's response of faith to the Father. In consequence, if the faith of believers is divorced from Christ's faith, we seem to end up with yet another permutation of humanity pulling itself up by its own bootstraps.[75]

The other key element in the doctrine of justification by faith is that Christ's sacrificial death opens the way for believers to be justified by faith. This brings us to the issue of how to understand "faith of Christ." While some understand Christ's faith to indicate Christ's obedience and thereby his sacrificial death,[76] the phrase may be more helpfully understood within the framework of participating in Christ. M. D. Hooker connects the phrase "faith of Christ" to Paul's "in Christ" theme. Echoing Ireneaus, Hooker comments, "Christ became what we are, in order that *in him*, we might become what he is."[77] For Hooker, since we are "in Christ" through Christ's work of interchange,[78] "faith of Christ" denotes Christ's faith, which becomes our faith as we are in him. S. K. Williams nuances the meaning of "faith of Christ" this way:

> "*Pistis Christou* [faith of Christ] is that faith which is characteristic of believers because they are 'in Christ.' . . . Believers' faith, like his, is the way of death (2:19) and 'new creation' (6:15). This faith, the very possibility and character of which derive from Christ's own, Paul calls *Pistis Christou.*"[79]

It must further be said that Christ's faith refers also to his humanity. While on occasion Paul refers to God's faithfulness (e.g., 1 Cor. 1:9; 10:13), faith is essentially a human action or disposition (e.g., Rom. 14:1, 22) and a most commendable one at that (e.g., Rom. 3:28). Paul may also be investing the word "faith" with its typical meaning of "proof." In the ancient world the Greek word *pistis* meant evidence that forms the basis on which belief is based.[80] Taking the phrase as an appositive genitive, it bears the meaning "proof that is Christ." Therefore the phrase "Christ's faith" refers to what Wallis calls "the fullness of the incarnate Son's humanity"[81] and to the proof of his identity. The character of Christ's faith gives evidence that he is the archetypal human being, while not diminishing his identity also as Son of God, Lord, and Christ. When believers are "in Christ" they participate in the archetypal human being Jesus Christ and so become righteous (cf. Rom. 5:15–19). This archetypal human being is Son of God and so has God's character—righteousness.[82] Faith in Christ allows believers to become righteous and faithful as Christ is.[83]

There is much more to say about the rich concepts and important issues found in Paul's letter to the Galatians, but these must wait for the commentary on individual verses. Yet, if this introduction has not adequately whetted the appetite for focused study of Galatians, perhaps the following general observation will help.

Spending time studying Paul is a corrective to viewing Christianity as the same as certain moral frameworks, or to equating particular cultural expressions, or even patriotism, with Christianity. Paul's argument against circumcision, which is an argument against identifying with a certain religious disposition and a particular nation, speaks to our current struggles to be shaped by Christ apart from inherited standards of behavior or national allegiance. Further, spending time studying Paul is a summons to be less attuned to the pressures and pleasures of our social context and more aware of the presence of Christ in our midst. Paul's attempt to put into words the fundamental importance of the profound and all-encompassing knowledge of being "in Christ" speaks to the possibility of living by faith, not achievement, in our time. Paul invites us to be molded not by inner needs or external circumstances, but to know freedom—the freedom of being "in Christ."

## Notes

1. Tacitus, *Hist.* 5.1–2 (Jackson, LCL).
2. Tacitus writes: "the Jews regard as profane all that we hold sacred; on the other hand, they permit all that we abhor" (ibid., 5.4). In speaking of the temple's fortifications he writes: "The founders of the city [Jerusalem] had foreseen that there would be many wars because

the ways of their people differed so from those of the neighbours" (ibid., 5.12). Tacitus charges the Jews with superstition (ibid., 5.1).

    3. Ibid., 5.5.

    4. *Against Apion* 2.154 (Thackeray, LCL).

    5. For evidence of "god-fearers," see A. Segal, *Paul the Convert: The Apostolate and Apostasy of Saul the Pharisee* (New Haven: Yale University Press, 1990), p. 94; and P. R. Trebilco, *Jewish Communities in Asia Minor* (Cambridge: Cambridge University Press, 1991), pp. 152–66. See M. Hengel and A. M. Schwemer for a discussion of the matter of pagan sympathizers to Judaism at the time of the birth of Christianity (*Paul between Damascus and Antioch: The Unknown Years* [trans. J. Bowden; Louisville, Ky.: Westminster John Knox, 1997], pp. 61–90).

    6. Juvenal, *Satires* 14.96–106 (Ramsay, LCL).

    7. John Chrysostom delivered sermons in the fourth century A.D. that testify to the fact that even after the Christian faith had existed for several generations, believers in Christ were powerfully drawn to Judaism. He declared: "I know that many have high regard for the Jews and they think that their present way of life is holy. That is why I am so anxious to uproot this deadly opinion." (*Homily 1 against the Jews* [Meeks and Wilken], p. 89.) Chrysostom speaks of those "sick with Judaism" "who belong to us and say that they believe in our teaching, [yet] attend their festivals, and even share in their celebrations and join in their feasts" (ibid., p. 86). See L. H. Feldman, who gives thirty-one reasons, including economic and social ones, why third-century Christians were still attracted to Judaism (*Jew and Gentile in the Ancient World: Attitudes and Interactions from Alexander to Justinian* [Princeton: Princeton University Press, 1993], pp. 369–89).

    8. *Dial.* 1 (*ANF* 1.194). Often the qualification "circumcised" was used with a strong sense of distaste. In one of his *Epigrams* the Roman poet Marcus Valerius Martial (ca. 40–103) addresses a Roman girl. He asks why no Roman is to her liking and yet she does not "shun the loins of circumcised Jews" (Martial, *Epigrams* 7.30 [Bailey, LCL]).

    9. It appears that Paul can accept Jewish Christians like Peter who follow Torah, but in accordance with Jesus' interpretation of it. Paul's use of the phrase *pistis Christou* in 2:15–16a affirms an understanding shared by a portion of early Jewish Christians: Jesus' faithfulness to the law defines law observance for those who follow him. For a similar understanding, see J. D. G. Dunn, "The New Perspective on Paul," in *Jesus, Paul and the Law: Studies in Mark and Galatians* (Louisville, Ky.: Westminster John Knox, 1990), pp. 183–205, esp. p. 189; idem, "The Incident at Antioch (Gal. 2:11–18)," in *Jesus, Paul and the Law,* 129–74, esp. p. 155; and B. W. Longenecker, *The Triumph of Abraham's God: The Transformation of Identity in Galatians* (Nashville: Abingdon, 1998), pp. 101–3. See also Additional Notes on 2:15–16.

10. See especially J. Munck, *Paul and the Salvation of Mankind* (London: SCM, 1959), pp. 130–34; and L. Gaston, *Paul and the Torah* (Vancouver: University of British Columbia Press, 1987), p. 81.

11. *The Kerygmata Petrou 1, The Epistle of Peter to James,* 2:112.

12. *The Kerygmata Petrou 2, Testimony regarding the Recipients of the Epistle,* 2:113 (Hennecke).

13. For a comprehensive bibliography on the subject and a good overview of various opinions on Paul's opponents and their relationship to the Jerusalem church, see R. N. Longenecker, *Galatians* (WBC 41; Dallas: Word, 1990), pp. lxxxviii–xcvi.

14. For a cogent critique of the hypothesis that there was substantial division between Paul and the Jerusalem leaders and that Paul's opponents acted under the authority of the Jerusalem church, see C. C. Hill, *Hellenists and Hebrews: Reappraising Division within the Earliest Church* (Minneapolis: Fortress, 1992).

15. For a particularly interesting reconstruction of the gospel that the rival evangelists may have preached see J. L. Martyn, "A Law-Observant Mission to Gentiles: The Background of Galatians," *SJT* 38 (1985), pp. 307–24.

16. For a presentation of five different Pauline chronologies based on trying to reconcile the account in Acts with that in Paul, see F. O. Francis and J. P. Sampley, eds., *Pauline Parallels* (2d ed.; Philadelphia: Fortress, 1984), pp. 67, 141, 175, 207, 223.

17. So Longenecker, *Galatians,* p. lxxii.

18. So J. C. Beker, *Paul the Apostle: The Triumph of God in Life and Thought* (Philadelphia: Fortress, 1980), p. 42; and J. L. Martyn, *Galatians* (AB 33A; Garden City, N.Y.: Doubleday, 1997), p. 16.

19. As noted by F. J. Matera, *Galatians* (Collegeville, Minn.: Liturgical Press, 1992), p. 24.

20. J. B. Lightfoot wrote: "The Epistle to Galatians stands in relation to the Roman letter, as the rough model to the finished statue" (*Saint Paul's Epistle to the Galatians* [London: Macmillan, 1910], p. 55). This has suggested to some that the letters were written within a relatively short space of time.

21. See Matera, who notes that some who hold to a north Galatian hypothesis date the letter early, whereas some who argue for a south Galatian destination date the letter later (*Galatians,* p. 20).

22. J. Knox in particular articulated the importance of distinguishing between the record of Paul in Acts, which is secondhand, and Paul's own account. Knox argued that since the letters are a firsthand account, where there is any discrepancy between Acts and Paul's letters, the letters are always to be taken as the true witness to events. He further argued that Luke's concerns undoubtedly affected his shaping of the story of Paul. Luke wanted to stress the centrality of Jerusalem, the importance of the Twelve, and the political innocuousness of Christianity. In

particular Luke's desire to stress the unity of a church centralized in Jerusalem affected both the order and manner of his record of Paul's activity. Knox suggests, for instance, that for the purpose of emphasizing the
harmony of the early church, Luke placed the Jerusalem Council of Acts
15 "earlier in Paul's career than it belongs" (*Chapters in a Life of Paul* [New
York: Abingdon, 1950], p. 67). See also G. Lüdemann (*Paul, Apostle to the
Gentiles: Studies in Chronology* [trans. F. S. Jones; Philadelphia: Fortress,
1984]), who uses the letters as primary evidence for constructing Paul's
chronology.

23. For instance, see D. Lührmann (*Galatians: A Continental Commentary* [trans. O. C. Dean Jr.; Minneapolis: Fortress, 1992], p. 3). J. Murphy-
O'Connor uses almost exclusively evidence from the letters in his dating
of Galatians (*Paul: A Critical Life* [Oxford: Clarendon, 1996], p. 182). H. D.
Betz puts it this way: "There is no real need to think that the author of
Acts always had reliable or complete information. . . . Hence, we are not
in the position to say with certainty on which of his journeys Paul
founded the churches" (*Galatians* [Hermeneia; Philadelphia: Fortress,
1979], pp. 4–5).

24. It must be said that even if we decided that the two passages
chronicled the same event, this would determine only that Galatians
was written after an event recorded both by Paul and Luke. It would not
tell us whether it came early or late in Paul's career. Just as in his gospel,
Luke may have ordered the events of Jesus' life to suit the purposes of
telling the story of Jesus in a particular way, so in Acts he may have arranged the events of Paul's life in order to correspond to his agenda.

25. Noting the difference between the way Peter and Paul are
presented in Acts and Galatians, F. C. Baur wrote: "The Acts passes over
the occurrence at Antioch with a resolute silence" (*The Church History of
the First Three Centuries* [trans. A. Menzies; vol. 1; London: Williams &
Norgate, 1878], p. 55).

26. These restrictions are often referred to as the Noachian commandments, that is, commandments applicable to both Jews and to
Gentiles living in contact with Jews. Depending upon how one translates "blood," it could refer to murder. For a judicious discussion of the
meaning of the decree see S. G. Wilson, *Luke and the Law* (Cambridge:
Cambridge University Press, 1983), esp. pp. 84–102.

27. For other comparisons of the Jerusalem Council with Gal. 2,
see K. F. Nickel, *The Collection: A Study in Paul's Strategy* (London: SCM,
1966), pp. 40–59; and Meeks and Wilken, *Jews and Christians in Antioch*,
pp. 16–18.

28. It should be noted that none of the other four visits to Jerusalem in Acts (9:26–27; 11:29–30; 12:25; 18:22; 21:15) are likely candidates
for referring to the visit Paul recounts in Gal. 2:1–10. Furthermore, Paul
describes his other Jerusalem visit so sparsely (Gal. 1:18–20) that it is impossible to relate it with any certainty to one of the visits in Acts. See,

however, C. J. Hemer, who thinks it possible to relate this visit to Acts 9 (*The Book of Acts in the Setting of Hellenistic History* [ed. C. H. Gempf; Tübingen: J. C. B. Mohr {Paul Siebeck}, 1989], p. 248).

29. This conclusion agrees substantially with that of Hill, *Hellenists and Hebrews*, p. 113.

30. See particularly D. M. Stanley, *Christ's Resurrection in Pauline Soteriology* (AnBib 13; Rome: Pontifical Biblical Institute, 1961), pp. 60–80; and C. Buck and G. Taylor, *Saint Paul: A Study in the Development of His Thought* (New York: Scribner's, 1969), pp. 82–102.

31. J. Knox, "On the Pauline Chronology: Buck-Taylor-Hurd Revisited," in *The Conversation Continues: Studies in Paul and John* (ed. R. T. Fortna and B. R. Gaventa; Nashville: Abingdon, 1990), pp. 258–74.

32. Knox, *Chapters in a Life of Paul*, esp. pp. 52–58.

33. If only on the basis of the collection project, the letter to the Romans should be viewed as later than 2 Corinthians. In Romans Paul states that he has finished his work in the east and now has his eyes on the western Mediterranean, whereas 2 Corinthians gives evidence that Paul is still involved in his missionary work in the east. Therefore, the change in the Galatian churches' participation most likely occurred between 1 and 2 Corinthians, with further evidence for this change being given in Romans.

34. As 2 Corinthians is widely recognized to be a composite of several of Paul's letters (see H. D. Betz, "Corinthians, Second Epistle to the," *ABD* 1:1148–54), it is possible that part of 2 Corinthians might precede 1 Corinthians. By and large, however, scholarship considers that 2 Corinthians contains letter fragments that were for the most part written after 1 Corinthians.

35. *Geography* 12.5.1 (Jones, LCL).

36. *The Celts in Anatolia and the Impact of Roman Rule*, vol. 1 of *Anatolia: Land, Men, and Gods in Asia Minor* (Oxford: Clarendon, 1993), p. 42.

37. *Deipnosophistae* 4.154b (Gulick, LCL).

38. Murphy-O'Connor, *Paul*, p. 190.

39. Ibid., pp. 189–90.

40. So Martyn, *Galatians*, p. 16.

41. Mitchell demonstrates that "a majority of the inhabitants of Asia Minor were in some measure bilingual in Greek and an indigenous language" (*The Celts in Anatolia*, p. 175), yet even up to the fourth century A.D. native Galatian words survived the influence of Greece and Rome, particularly in rural areas (ibid., p. 50). This suggests that there would have been a greater number of Greek speakers in the more urban south than in the north. Nevertheless, a case based simply on the distribution of the Greek language cannot be conclusively made.

42. See esp. W. M. Ramsay, *A Historical Commentary on St. Paul's Epistle to the Galatians* (London: Hodder & Stoughton, 1900), p. 160.

43. The lack of a Jewish population is noted by Martyn, who uses this as evidence for a northern destination (*Galatians*, p. 16, n. 11).

44. Cf. S. K. Williams, *Galatians* (Abingdon New Testament Commentaries; Nashville: Abingdon, 1997), p. 21.

45. *The Rise of the Church*, vol. 2 of *Anatolia*, p. 4.

46. See L. H. Schiffman, *Who Was a Jew? Rabbinic and Halakhic Perspectives on the Jewish-Christian Schism* (Hoboken, N.J.: Ktav, 1985), esp. pp. 9–17.

47. *Paul and Rabbinic Judaism: Some Rabbinic Elements in Pauline Theology* (4th ed.; Philadelphia: Fortress, 1980), p. 321.

48. Ibid., p. xxx.

49. *Paul the Apostle*, p. 343.

50. Ibid., p. 345.

51. Knox, *Chapters in a Life of Paul*, pp. 135–36.

52. *Paul the Convert*, p. 34.

53. Ibid., p. 11.

54. Ibid., p. 33.

55. Ibid., p. xii.

56. *Paul, the Law and the Jewish People* (Philadelphia: Fortress, 1983), p. 207.

57. Ibid., 178.

58. *Paul and Palestinian Judaism* (Philadelphia: Fortress, 1977), p. 552.

59. Ibid., 551–52.

60. "Paul, Classical Anti-Jewish Polemic, and the Letter to the Romans," in *Self-Definition and Self-Discovery in Early Christianity: A Study in Changing Horizons* (ed. D. J. Hawkin and T. Robinson; Lewiston, N.Y.: Edwin Mellen Press, 1990; Studies in the Bible and Early Christianity, vol. 26, pp. 181–223), p. 207.

61. Recognized particularly by Beker, *Paul the Apostle;* and Segal, *Paul the Convert.*

62. Segal's suggestion that what became known as *Merkabah* mysticism is similar to Paul's identification between the believer and Christ is not, in fact, an adequate parallel to Paul's talk about being "in Christ" (*Paul the Convert*, p. 11). Such mysticism was reserved for what Segal calls "certain heroes" (p. 43), whereas Paul regards all believers as incorporated into Christ. Moreover, the apocalyptic and mystical literature to which Segal points speaks of the possibility of ascending to God's presence (p. 64) rather than, as in Paul, living both in the body and in Christ.

63. T. L. Donaldson has a similar understanding of Paul's loyalty to his kinfolk (*Paul and the Gentiles: Remapping the Apostle's Convictional World* [Minneapolis: Fortress, 1997], esp. p. 306). Donaldson further considers that the "Gentile triumphalism" that resulted from Paul's gospel ran counter to Paul's "conscious intentions," which were to be able to hold on to "two conflicting definitions of 'Israel' "—one historic Israel, the other Israel defined "in Christ" (ibid, p. 305).

64. Judaism and Christianity are still divided over this, of course. As G. Scholem puts it in the introduction to his excellent work on the history of the messianic idea in rabbinic Judaism, "any discussion of . . . Messianism is a delicate matter, for it is here that the essential conflict between Judaism and Christianity has developed and continues to exist" (*The Messianic Idea in Judaism* [New York: Schocken, 1971], p. 1).

65. See N. Dahl's cogent argument that Paul primarily used "Christ" as a proper name. Among his reasons are that in Paul "Christ" is never used predicatively, that is, Paul never says "Jesus is the Christ" ("The Messiahship of Jesus in Paul," in *The Crucified Messiah and Other Essays* [Minneapolis: Augsburg, 1974], pp. 37–47, esp. p. 37). "Paul represented a strikingly advanced stage in the evolution that transformed *Christos* from a messianic designation to Jesus' second proper name" (p. 41). Note the comment by Hengel and Schwemer that "in the Greek-speaking world [Christ] became a proper name with amazing rapidity" (*Paul between Damascus and Antioch,* p. 101).

66. We might contrast Paul's use of the designation "Christ" with that of Luke, who regularly uses it to mean Messiah, e.g., Acts 3:18; 5:42.

67. A. Schweitzer, *The Mysticism of Paul the Apostle* (trans. W. Montgomery; London: A & C Black, 1931), p. 377.

68. *Paul and Palestinian Judaism,* p. 549.

69. See especially E. R. Goodenough, "Paul and the Hellenization of Christianity," in *Religions in Antiquity* (ed. J. Neusner; Leiden: Brill, 1967), pp. 35–80; Longenecker, *Galatians,* pp. 87–88; R. B. Hays, *The Faith of Jesus Christ: An Investigation of the Narrative Substructure of Galatians 3:1–4:11* (Chico, Calif.: Scholars, 1983); idem, "PISTIS and Pauline Christology: What Is at Stake?" *SBL Seminar Papers, 1991* (SBLSP 30; Atlanta: Scholars, 1991), pp. 714–29; and I. G. Wallis, *The Faith of Jesus Christ in Early Christian Traditions* (SNTSMS 84; ed. M. E. Thrall; Cambridge: Cambridge University Press, 1995).

70. "Faithfulness and 'Faith,' " *Theology* 58 (1955), pp. 373–79.

71. "One Aspect of the Biblical Conception of Faith," *Expository Times* 68 (1957), pp. 111–14.

72. *The Semantics of Biblical Language* (Oxford: Oxford University Press, 1961), pp. 161–205.

73. Ibid., p. 175.

74. For a case in favor of the objective genitive reading, based largely on grammar, see A. J. Hulgren, "The *Pistis Christou* Formulation in Paul," *NovT* 22 (1980), pp. 248–63. For the opposite opinion see S. K. Williams, "Again *Pistis Christou,*" *CBQ* 49 (1987), pp. 431–47.

75. *The Faith of Jesus Christ in Early Christian Tradition,* p. 220.

76. So R. N. Longenecker, "The Obedience of Christ in the Theology of the Early Church," in *Reconciliation and Hope* (ed. R. Banks; Exeter: Paternoster, 1974), pp. 142–52; and Hays, "PISTIS and Pauline Christology."

77. See Hooker, "PISTIS XRISTOU," *NTS* 35 (1989), pp. 321–42, esp. pp. 337–39.

78. "Interchange and Suffering," in *Suffering and Martyrdom in the New Testament: Studies Presented to G. M. Styler* (ed. W. Horbury and B. McNeil; Cambridge: Cambridge University Press, 1981), pp. 70–83, esp. p. 70.

79. *Galatians*, pp. 69–70. Williams also writes: "When Paul speaks of *pistis Christou*, he has in mind that faith which is given its distinctive character by the absolute trust and unwavering obedience of Jesus, who created, in the last days, this mode of being human in the world" ("Again *Pistis Christou*," p. 446).

80. See D. M. Hay, "*Pistis* as 'Ground for Faith' in Hellenized Judaism and Paul," *JBL* 108 (1989), pp. 461–76.

81. *The Faith of Jesus Christ in Early Christian Traditions*, p. 220.

82. For a discussion of the meaning of "righteousness of God" as referring to God's character, see L. Ann Jervis, "Becoming Like God Through Christ: Romans," in *Patterns of Discipleship in the New Testament* (ed. R. N. Longenecker; Grand Rapids: Eerdmans, 1996), pp. 143–62, esp. pp. 155–61.

83. Throughout his letters Paul speaks of the consequences of participating in Christ, describing believers as becoming faithful (see 1 Cor. 7:25), sharing a spirit of faith (2 Cor. 4:13), and able to participate completely in the drama of Christ's humanity (i.e., faith), death (Gal. 2:20), and resurrection (2 Cor. 4:13–14).

## §1 Identification of the Senders and the Addressees and a Wish for Grace and Peace (Gal. 1:1–5)

**1:1** / As in all of his letters **Paul** begins by identifying himself as the sender. In ancient times a letter typically began with the writer's self-identification, and the opening commonly continued by naming the addressees and wishing them good health.

In Paul's letters, this typical wish is replaced by a wish for grace and peace. In the opening of Paul's letter to the Galatian churches, as in most of his other letters, Paul identifies himself as an **apostle** (cf. Rom. 1:1; 1 Cor. 1:1; 2 Cor. 1:1; and, if Pauline authorship is accepted, Eph. 1:1 and Col. 1:1). In Galatians Paul places his name in direct relation to his self-designation as apostle and then immediately goes on to qualify what kind of apostle he is. Often at the beginning of a letter Paul qualifies his apostleship as being by the will of God. In Galatians Paul makes a similar point in a particularly graphic and emphatic way, by describing the means by which he became an apostle and the identity of the one who called him: the source of his life's work is Jesus Christ and God the Father. And so Paul stresses that he is an apostle **sent not from men nor by man.** Paul's inclusion of both the plural and singular emphasizes that his apostleship did not originate from either a human group or an individual.

Paul represents himself to the Galatian churches as an apostle who acts on the highest authority, that of the risen Jesus Christ and God the Father. Among Paul's letters, the emphasis that divine authority undergirds his apostleship is most pronounced in his Galatian letter, even in contrast to Romans, where Paul also takes pains to underscore his apostleship (Rom. 1:1–6). In Galatians he is concerned to present himself as one whose apostolic function has divine authentication. Paul is sent by Jesus Christ and God the Father—by those whose authority and power the Galatian believers have already accepted.

In Galatians, unlike the other letter openings, Paul says that the one who called him is not only God (cf. 1 Cor. 1:1; 2 Cor. 1:1; Eph. 1:1; Col. 1:1) but also **Jesus Christ.** This unusual reference to Jesus Christ in connection with the authentication of his apostleship suggests that Paul wants to prove to his readers that he has the authority to preach the gospel of Christ (cf. 1:7) to them and to shape their life of faith in accordance with that gospel. Paul maintains a focus on Jesus Christ in the following verses which continues to function to validate his apostleship. Furthermore, Paul's description of the one who called him—**God the Father, who raised** [Jesus] **from the dead**—stands out from Paul's other letter openings. Here Paul appeals to the current faith of the Galatians who worship God as Father (cf. 1:3 and 4:6) and believe that he raised Jesus. Throughout this letter Paul speaks little about the resurrected Jesus Christ, stressing instead that Jesus Christ is the crucified one. The reference to Christ's resurrection is to an aspect of the faith that Paul knows his hearers are convinced of. The one who sends Paul to preach is the one who has the highest authority in the Galatian community—God the Father who raised Jesus Christ from the dead.

God was spoken of as a "Father" in both the Greek world in which Paul missionized (Zeus was referred to as "father") and the Jewish thought world that shaped his gospel (e.g., Isa. 63:16; Jer. 3:4; 31:9). Thus, the apostle seems to have found it a particularly useful appellation for God. He uses it in all of his opening addresses, usually in the context of his wish for peace (e.g., 2 Thess. 1:2; Phil. 1:2). At times Paul refers to the fatherhood of God in relation to Jesus (e.g., Rom. 15:6; 2 Cor. 1:3; 11:31), but in this case, since 1:3 refers to God as "our father," it appears that Paul means God as the father of those who believe in Jesus Christ. The emphasis on God as father at the opening of the letter (1:1, 3–4) signals that one of the concerns Paul will address is that of inheritance and sonship (3:15–4:7).

**1:2** / In all Pauline letters except Romans Paul identifies co-senders. In Galatians Paul says that the letter comes from himself and **all the brothers with me.** Paul's reference to an anonymous but substantial group of co-senders emphasizes the credibility of his own voice; he wants to communicate that the letter has the endorsement of a significant number of believers (cf. 1:8).

The letter's address **to the churches in Galatia** is remarkably sparse. The addresses of Paul's other letters typically include an affirmative statement such as "to all God's beloved at Rome" or "to the church of God which is at Corinth, to those sanctified in Christ Jesus, called to be saints" (Rom. 1:7; 1 Cor. 1:2, RSV). Rather than affirming his converts, Paul's terse address helps to set the tone for his letter. Paul writes not warmly but reproachfully. He clearly cannot commend his converts' faith. The absence of his usual commendation, combined with the stress in v. 1 on his apostolic credibility, suggests that Paul writes Galatians in an admonitionary tone.

The letter's address to "the churches" suggests that it was intended to be circulated among various groups of believers in the Roman province of Galatia. This sets it apart from Paul's other letters, which are typically written to a single church. It also indicates that the problem that Paul is combatting has spread among his various Galatian churches.

**1:3–5** / The wish for **grace and peace** is a standard feature of Paul's letters. Unlike the address, this feature is usually quite straightforward, saying simply, as in Romans, "grace and peace to you from God our Father and from the Lord Jesus Christ" (Rom. 1:7b). In Galatians Paul expands the wish to include a reference to the work of Jesus Christ: Christ **gave himself for our sins to rescue us from the present evil age.** Before launching into the difficult task of persuading his converts that they are being tempted to believe a false gospel, Paul uses this portion of the letter opening to stress the common faith he shares with his readers.

While **Lord** is a standard designation for Jesus Christ in Paul's opening wish for grace and peace (e.g., Rom. 1:7; 1 Cor. 1:3; 2 Cor. 1:2; Phil. 1:2), it may also have been particularly useful in the Galatian situation in which Paul is seeking to communicate with Gentile converts under the influence of Jewish Christian missionaries. Greek-speaking Jews referred to God as Lord (e.g., Deut. 6:4), but there is little evidence for Greek religion referring to God as Lord. This suggests that Paul here, as elsewhere (e.g., Rom. 10:9; 1 Cor. 7:22; 12:3; Phil. 2:11), refers to Jesus Christ's divinity in a manner that originated in the earliest Jewish Christian communities. By initially describing the faith in terms with which his readers would feel comfortable—either because it is the way he introduced the faith to them or as a result of influences subsequent to his departure—Paul hopes to gain a hearing.

Several distinctive features of this passage can be attributed to Paul's tactic to resonate with what he thinks his readers accept. Only here in all of Paul's existing writings does he use the verb **rescue** *(exaireō);* only here does Paul directly apply the adjective "evil" to the present age; and the idea of the present age occurs only this once in Galatians. At this point Paul may be including or alluding to a confession of faith familiar to the Galatians. We see him doing something similar at the beginning of Romans (1:2–4).

It is difficult to determine whether this is a formulation of the faith that the Galatians received from Paul or whether it is one they had been taught by the rival evangelists. A strongly Jewish flavor might indicate that it originated with the rival evangelists.

The reference to sins on its own is not enough to suggest a Jewish provenance. Other ancients, apart from the Jews, recognized that human beings were caught in a struggle with what was commonly called their passions. Pagans turned to religion and philosophy in search of freedom from the passions. The challenge was to find a way to be freed from bondage to the passions and so to achieve god-like peace. Such a goal was understood as important for individuals and for society. Plutarch wrote:

> a city without holy places and gods, without any observance of prayers, oaths, oracles . . . might rather be formed without the ground it stands on than a government, once you remove all religion from under it. . . . It is this belief [which is] the underpinning and base that holds all society and legislation together. (*Reply to Colotes in Defence of the Other Philosophers* 1125E [Einarson and DeLacy, LCL])

Nonetheless, the word "sins" occurs in the phrase "for our sins," which is a clear reference to the Jewish idea of atonement. Another Jewish concept in this passage is that of rescue from the present evil age. This appeals to Jewish apocalyptic categories in which there is a distinction between this age and the age to come. On balance this description of the faith has a Jewish texture.

The question is, does it reflect Paul the Jew's understanding of the faith or the Jewish rival evangelists'? Certainly Paul elsewhere uses the ideas of atonement and apocalyptic ages. Paul refers to Jesus as one who "was delivered over to death for our sins" (Rom. 4:25), and describes this age as transitory (1 Cor. 2:6) and characterized by blindness to God (1 Cor. 2:8). Yet the formulation in this passage differs both from Paul's normal allusions to these Jewish concepts (this is the only time Paul connects Christ's death, as opposed to his return at the last day, with believers' being rescued from the "present evil age"), and from the rest of the letter, which does not refer overtly to apocalyptic concepts. The formulation thus appears to have originated with Paul's rivals in Galatia. Paul adopts some of the features of his opponents' formulation in order to gain an ear with those in Galatia who are convinced by the alternate gospel. He recognizes that unless he speaks something of their language they will not hear him.

The closing words of this affirmation of faith—**to whom be the glory for ever and ever. Amen**—suggest that Paul meant to convey a worship tone. His inclusion of the word "amen" is in effect an invitation to the Galatians to agree with him by responding "amen."

---

## Additional Notes §1

---

**1:1** / For information on and examples of ancient Greek letters, see J. L. White, *Light from Ancient Letters* (Philadelphia: Fortress, 1986).

It should be noted that Paul accepts the apostleship of those who were before him (1:17), for instance, Peter and James (1:18–19), who may have validated their apostolic commission on the basis of having known Jesus personally. Paul considers that apostles share in common a commitment to evangelize (2:8) and that in one way or another they have seen the Lord (1 Cor. 9:1).

**1:5** / We might compare this passage with another in Paul—Rom. 11:36. We might also compare it to one in Virgil's *Aeneid*, where priests are worshiping the glorious acts of Hercules by saying "Oh, unconquerable! You are the slayer by your own might of those cloud-born creatures of two shapes in one, Hylaeus and Phlous, and also the monstrous Cretan Bull, and the gigantic lion under Nemea's rock. You shocked the lake of Styx into trembling" (7.293–94; trans. Jackson Knight, pp. 209–10]. By inviting his readers to share in the atmosphere of worship, Paul fosters a sense of unity or shared experience before beginning his admonishments.

**1:6–9** / Paul's abrupt expression of astonishment—**I am
astonished**—right after the letter opening (1:1–5) signals, like his
his terse address (1:2b), that he is seriously concerned about his
converts. He wastes no time pretending otherwise. At this junc-
ture in Paul's letters, after the wish for grace and peace, Paul
typically gives thanks to God for the faith of the recipients of his
letter (see Rom. 1:8; 1 Cor. 1:4; Phil. 1:3; 1 Thess. 1:2; 2 Thess. 1:3;
Phlm. 4) or blesses God (2 Cor. 1:3). Galatians stands out because
there is no thanksgiving or blessing and also because of these
words, "I am astonished." Paul opens the main body of his letter
by pronouncing judgment on the Galatian believers' willingness
to believe a gospel other than the one he preached to them.

Paul chooses the strong word **deserting** (*metatithesthe*) to signal
to the Galatian believers that their reception of the rival evangelists'
message is equivalent to becoming apostates. The same Greek
word occurs in 2 Maccabees 7:24, where it refers to "turning from
the ways of one's fathers." The word here is in the present tense,
indicating that the action is ongoing, with particular stress on the
present—the Galatians are turned away from the one who has
called them, and their present life demonstrates their choice.

Paul charges that the Galatian believers are deserting the
very one who **called** them (cf. 5:8). He begins his rebuke by focusing on their relationship with God. In their **turning to a different
gospel** they are transferring their allegiance away from the one
who wanted to deliver them from the present evil age. The
Galatian believers and Paul know themselves to be called by
grace (1:15), and Paul appeals to the Galatians' understanding of
themselves as those who have been called **by the grace of Christ**—a
grace that resulted in their being rescued (v. 4). The phrase
"grace of Christ" refers to the gospel in a nutshell, in a manner
similar to his statement in 3:1b. Christ's gift of himself in his cru-

cifixion is central to the gospel Paul preached and in which the Galatians believed. Paul is incredulous that they are turning toward a different gospel. In rejecting his gospel they are also rejecting the one who called them through Paul's gospel—God.

Paul uses one Greek word for "different" in the phrase **different gospel** (*heteron,* v. 6) and another word also meaning "different" *(allo)* in the phrase translated **really no gospel at all** (v. 7). Some scholars have argued that the word in verse 6 has the nuance of "difference within the same kind," whereas the one in verse 7 has the sense of "difference of kind." Paul's use of these two words meaning "different" in 1 Corinthians 15:39–41 is taken as evidence for such an interpretation. It is possible that Paul had this nuance in mind, in which case in verse 6 he would be appealing to the Galatians' conviction that they thought they were adopting a variation of the gospel, whereas, as he says in verse 7, they are trying to find something that does not exist—another gospel. There is, according to Paul, only one gospel.

Paul then turns the spotlight onto those who are **trying to pervert the gospel of Christ.** His ire at the opening of the letter is directed toward those who are teaching the Galatians that there is another gospel. Paul does not name the troublemakers here or anywhere throughout the letter. This may be either because he does not know their names or because he does not want to dignify them by naming them. The discrepancy about whether Paul is concerned with one (1:8, 9) or a number of opponents (e.g., 1:7) is probably due to the context in which his opponents are mentioned. There were a number of them, but when Paul wishes to clarify the problem they cause he focuses on the offense of one person, perhaps to locate the trouble in a single opponent whom he, the true apostle, stands over against.

When Paul first identifies the people behind the false teaching he describes them as people who **are throwing you into confusion.** Their intention is that of "trying to pervert" the gospel of Christ. The Greek word for "pervert" (*metastrepsai*) has the sense of changing from one thing or state to another. In this context, in which Paul thinks of his gospel as that which is good, the sense of distortion or change for the worse is given.

The idea of change dominates verses 6–7. Paul's own life demonstrates that he is not afraid of change, but he thinks the changes that the Galatian converts are making are dangerous. Paul feels so strongly that his gospel must not be changed that he says that anyone who proclaims **a gospel other than** Paul's—

even if it is Paul himself, one of those with him, or an **angel** out of heaven—should be accursed. Paul further underlines this point by self-consciously repeating himself in verse 9, using almost the same wording. In verse 9 he moves from a future to a real present condition: someone is proclaiming a gospel contrary to that which the Galatians **accepted.** The Galatians already gave their allegiance to the gospel Paul preached, and Paul warns them not to change.

Paul refers to his original preaching in which he **already said** that the Galatians were not to believe anything other than what they were told by Paul. This may suggest that even at the first Paul knew his gospel would be opposed. The first person plural might be Paul's way of referring to himself, which he goes on to do (1:11). At other places in his letters Paul uses the first person plural self-referentially (e.g., 1 Thess. 2:18).

Twice Paul curses the one who is preaching a **gospel other than the one we preached to you.** Paul's solemn curse (**let him be eternally condemned,** vv. 8–9) indicates how serious a deception he believes is being perpetrated on the Galatians. Someone who preaches this false gospel can deserve only eternal damnation. There is only one gospel—the gospel of Christ that Paul preached and they believed. Paul reminds the Galatians that they have already been told, presumably in his missionary preaching, that they should not give credence to any gospel other than the one they accepted. Paul's equating of his gospel with the gospel of Christ is another way to impugn the rival evangelists' message.

Paul seems to expect that his hearers will know what he means when he refers to the "gospel," which suggests that he may have characterized his message this way when he was with them. Christians very early on could hear the word "gospel" and invest it with a range and depth of meaning. The word must have connoted for them the story of Jesus' life, death, resurrection, and the salvific significance of that story for those who believe. When Paul refers to the gospel of Christ (v. 7) he emphasizes that what he preaches is Christ's gospel; in this way he affirms that there is no gospel but the one the Galatians heard from him.

Furthermore, he sets up a contrast not only between his opponents' gospel and his own but also between the opponents' gospel and the Galatians' previous stance in which they accepted his gospel. In verse 9 Paul reminds the Galatians that they have received as true his gospel, thereby underscoring first that to turn to a different gospel is to turn away from what they have already accepted and second that if they already know his to be true, it is self-evident that the rival evangelists' gospel cannot be combined with the one they accepted from him.

**1:10** / Paul continues in verse 10 by defending himself against what is likely a charge against him—that he is a people pleaser. Those who have come into his churches to teach that observance of the law is essential may have been presenting Paul's law-free gospel as a sign of his weakness, saying that he wanted to make the gospel as palatable as possible and so to **win the approval of men.** Paul says to the contrary that he is **a servant of Christ.** This, as he makes clear at the end of the letter (6:17), is not a role that curries favor with people but rather it entails suffering. Paul insists that he is not one to bend his shape in order to gain favor from others, saying that what he has just **now** said proves that he cares only about the truth. He implies that his former way of being did concern itself with **trying to please men** but now being a "servant of Christ" makes such a stance impossible. For Paul, serving Christ is about only being for the gospel. As his gospel is not of human origin it will be offensive or discomfiting to people.

In other letters as well (1 Thess. 2:4) Paul claims that his focus is on pleasing God. In some instances Paul says that pleasing other people is appropriate (1 Cor. 10:33), but concerning the integrity of his gospel Paul sees things in either/or terms. To be a servant of Christ is mutually exclusive of pleasing people.

In the opening of his letter (1:1–10) Paul has emphasized the divine origin of his apostleship (1:1), signalled his disapproval of the current faith of his converts (1:2b), expressed his bewilderment at their actions (1:6–7), denounced his rivals (1:8–9), and taken umbrage at unfair criticisms of himself. Before we modern readers even know exactly what Paul is upset about, we know beyond a shadow of a doubt that the apostle's emotions are raw as he writes to his Galatian churches.

---

### Additional Notes §2

---

**1:6** / The Greek word for **I am astonished** *(thaumazō)* is probably carefully chosen, as it was a standard expression used by Greek letter writers of the time to indicate "incredulity and dissatisfaction" (so White, *Light from Ancient Letters,* p. 208).

**1:9** / **Preaching** *(euangelizetai)* is a cognate verb to the noun "gospel" *(euangelion).*

## §3 The Credibility of the Gospel Paul Proclaims (Gal. 1:11–12)

**1:11–12** / Paul continues his self-defense by focusing on the gospel itself. This is Paul's usual way of underscoring his authority and credibility. For instance, at the beginning of Romans—a letter in which Paul wishes, among other things, to encourage the Roman believers to accept his apostolic authority—Paul highlights his understanding of and commitment to the gospel (Rom. 1:1–6). At the start of Galatians Paul also turns his hearers' attention to the gospel. Paul was so thoroughly identified with the gospel he preached, both in his own mind and in the minds of others, that the most direct way to establish his credibility was to argue for the truth of the gospel he proclaimed. This focus explains why he now uses the first person singular "I" when talking about the preaching of the gospel, whereas before he had used the first person plural "we" (vv. 8–9). The issue he wishes to address for the sake of his hearers is the connection between his own trustworthiness and that of the gospel he preached to them. Furthermore, the way the semantic rhythm and rhetorical intention of verses 11–12 echo verse 1 suggests again that to Paul the issue of his apostolic credibility is one with the issue of the credibility of the gospel.

Paul affirms that the gospel he preached **is not something that man made up,** as proven by the fact that he did not receive it from a human being but rather **by revelation from Jesus Christ.** His gospel is therefore above criticism, and so it cannot be changed or added to, even by an angel from heaven. This is also why Paul himself, as the preacher of the gospel, should be trusted.

## Additional Note §3

**1:12** / **I received it by revelation from Jesus Christ:** In v. 17 the apostle says he "returned to Damascus," which would suggest that this experience of God revealing God's Son to Paul took place in Damascus (cf. Acts 9). The Greek for the phrase "by revelation from Jesus Christ" can mean either that Jesus Christ is the content of the revelation or that he is the bringer of the revelation. In connection with v. 16a it might seem most reasonable to opt for the former reading—that the substance of the revelation was Jesus Christ (so F. F. Bruce, *The Epistle to the Galatians* [The New International Greek Testament Commentary; Grand Rapids: Eerdmans, 1982], p. 89). In connection with v. 1, with which vv. 11–12 have semantic resonances, it seems appropriate to understand Jesus Christ as the means by which the revelation was given to Paul (so Longenecker, *Galatians*, p. 24). Perhaps the phrase should be understood in both ways at once: Jesus Christ is the content and the bringer of the gospel. Paul's apostleship came through Jesus Christ (v. 1), and the gospel revealed to him was about Jesus Christ (v. 16). The revelation he speaks of in v. 12, then, concerns both content and means.

## §4 Paul's Apostolic Credibility and His Relationship to the Jerusalem Church (Gal. 1:13–17)

**1:13–14** / And now Paul turns to himself directly, apparently defending himself against criticisms of his past relationship to the Christian movement and particularly to important Christian persons in Jerusalem. Paul begins by reiterating his dramatic call: he went from being one who **persecuted the church of God and tried to destroy it** to one who preached the very message he had been trying to quash. His use of the word "destroy" stresses that in his former life his actions against the church were exceptionally violent and that he had intended to obliterate it. The Galatians are aware of Paul's **previous way of life.** The Greek does not tell us whether the Galatians heard about his former manner of life from him on his evangelistic visit or from others subsequent to his departure from Galatia. Either way, the emphasis on **my** in the Greek gives the impression that Paul takes full responsibility for his previous conduct and does not intend to hide it.

Paul describes himself as one who was **extremely zealous for the traditions** of Judaism but who, in a dramatic turnabout, responded to a call to preach Christ "among the Gentiles" (v. 16). 

Paul describes his former life as being within **Judaism** (see also v. 14), suggesting that he sees his faith in Christ as separate from the religion into which both he and Christ were born. Some Greek Jewish writers referred to their religion as Judaism (e.g., 2 Macc. 2:21; 8:1; 14:38; 4 Macc. 4:26), but this is not Paul's normal designation for his religious heritage. By describing the various groups of Christian believers as one entity—the church of God—he further clarifies the distinction between his present and former religious worlds.

Paul boasts that he exceeded others of his age in being zealous for the traditions of his **fathers.** The phrase "traditions of my fathers" was a common one in both Jewish and pagan ancient writers. Respect for previous traditions was a bulwark of ancient society, and it was a noble thing to be zealous for the traditions. In the face of criticisms that he waters down the faith by not requiring Gentiles to be circumcised and follow Torah, Paul states in effect that his present stance is not because he is either incapable or ignorant of following Torah.

**1:15–17** / Paul roots his conversion in **God,** who determined his role as preacher to the Gentiles from birth. This concept of his having been **set apart** or appointed also occurs elsewhere in Paul, particularly at Romans 1:1. Paul thinks of his ministry as divinely ordained.

The Greek of the phrase "set me apart from birth" *(ho aphorisas me ek koilias mētros mou)* can be read to express the idea that the setting apart was from the time when Paul was conceived in his mother's womb. This concept was part of prophetic self-understanding (cf. Jer. 1:5). The idea that a person or place could be set apart by God for a special purpose is intrinsic to the Jewish religious mind. The prophets, for instance, were understood to be specially designated by God (Deut. 18:15) so that they could speak on behalf of God (Deut. 18:18). Mount Sinai (Exod. 19:23) and the temple (Ezek. 45:1–4) were places that were understood to be set apart as holy.

The apostle's conversion was also a commission to preach Christ **among the Gentiles,** or as the Greek *(en tois ethnesin)* can also be translated, "among the nations." Paul's designation of his gospel as one for the nations occurs chiefly in Galatians (here and at Gal. 2:2, 8–9) and Romans. Both letters include a reference to the story of Abraham (e.g., Gal. 3:6–14; 4:22–23; Rom. 4:1–25). Regardless of whether Paul refers to Abraham in Galatians because his opponents had introduced the patriarch into the discussion, Paul was able to find a very useful complex of ideas in the Abraham story. Particularly helpful are the notions that Abraham's call was to be a great nation (Gen. 12:2), that God promised Abraham he would be the "father of many nations" (Gen. 17:4), and that "through [Abraham's] offspring all nations on earth will be blessed" (Gen. 22:18). Paul makes the connection between these offspring of Abraham and those of Christ (3:16) and understands his missionary sphere as being among those whom God promised God would eventually bless through the offspring of Abraham. Paul's description of himself as one sent to

preach among the Gentiles/nations is rich with meaning for one
so steeped in the traditions of his ancestors.

Whereas elsewhere Paul speaks of non-Jews as Greeks
(e.g., Gal. 2:3; Rom. 1:16), here he speaks of them as Gentiles.
"Gentile" was a Jewish designation for non-Jews and so more
than likely the one used by the rival evangelists. At this point
Paul may be echoing his opponents so as to resonate with and
then reshape the Galatians' current sensibilities.

Paul affirms that as soon as God called him he separated
himself from Judaism so completely that he did not even go to
see those Jews who had become believers in Jesus. Paul's claim of
independence from the Jerusalem church may be a subtle slight
to the Jerusalem church, which has not separated from Judaism.
Part of his agenda in 2:1–10 is to demonstrate that the church at
Jerusalem has problems. There are "false brothers" and a lack of
agreement.

Paul's purpose in describing his conversion experience
goes beyond underscoring his credentials as an apostle for the
gospel. He says **I did not consult any man** and elaborates: he did
not **go up to Jerusalem to see those who were apostles before** he
was. Paul reiterates (v. 12) that the gospel he preached to the
Galatians was not influenced by human teaching. He now wants
to make it particularly clear that it was not even influenced by
the views of the Jerusalem believers. Perhaps one of the criticisms of Paul made by the troublemakers in Galatia was that at
one point he had accepted the teaching of the Jerusalem church
but now, in "trying to please men" (v. 10), he has softened his
gospel for the purpose of extending his influence among Gentiles. Paul makes clear that his conversion was an experience un-
tainted by human intervention, that his commission came to him
at that moment, and that subsequent to this remarkable experience he was not in contact with the Jerusalem church. The gospel
he preached to the Galatians is the unadulterated gospel, bearing no signs of influence from any human source, not even that
of Jerusalem Christianity.

## Additional Notes §4

**1:13** / Where did Paul persecute the church? As he refers to persecuting the church in parallelism to advancing in Judaism (1:14) it is most likely that this occurred in Jerusalem (cf. Hengel and Schwemer, *Paul between Damascus and Antioch*, p. 37), the city to which a zealous Jew would go in order to study Torah. Note also that in 1 Thess. 2:15 there is evidence for the churches in Judea (not Syria) being persecuted.

**1:16** / The designation of Jesus as God's **Son** was one of the earliest Christian descriptions of Jesus. The pre-Pauline confession in Rom. 1:2–4 gives evidence that at the beginning of the faith Jesus was understood to be God's Son.

For a discussion of the meaning of "Son of God" in the OT, Greek, Hellenistic, and Hellenistic Jewish literature, see M. Hengel, *The Son of God: The Origin of Christology in the History of Jewish-Hellenistic Religion* (trans. J. Bowden; Philadelphia: Fortress, 1976), pp. 21–56. See also the excellent overview by J. Fossum on "Son of God" in *ABD* 6:128–37.

Some scholars have suggested that the phrase translated **in me** points to the inwardness of Paul's conversion experience (so Bruce, *Galatians*, p. 93). In favor of understanding Paul as speaking of an internal visionary experience is the fact that he uses a comparable phrase in 2:20 and 4:6 (so H. D. Betz, *Galatians* [Hermeneia; Philadelphia: Fortress, 1979], p. 71; cf. Longenecker, *Galatians*, p. 32). Yet there follows a corresponding expression in Greek that reads lit. "in order that I might preach him *in* the Gentiles," which suggests that the first phrase might be better translated as "to me." Paul is primarily concerned with the fact that he received a revelation rather than with how he received it, and the chief consequence of the revelation was his commission to preach God's Son to the Gentiles. Paul gives no record of his vision such as Acts does; instead the focus is on the task given him (see J. D. G. Dunn, " 'A Light to the Gentiles': The Significance of the Damascus Road Christophany for Paul," in *The Glory of Christ in the New Testament* [Oxford: Clarendon, 1987], pp. 251–68).

**1:17** / **Arabia:** Paul does not say whether he preached when he was in Arabia or cogitated on his conversion experience. Usually, as J. Knox notes, "it is . . . supposed that he went for solitude and meditation" (*Chapters in a Life of Paul*, p. 77). Yet, as Paul tells of his call and commission, it sounds as if he knew immediately that he was to preach to Gentiles. This might lead us to suppose that when he went to Arabia he did so as a missionary. Ambrosiaster surmised that Paul went to Arabia because he knew no one else had yet gone there: "Therefore he set out from Damascus to Arabia to preach where there was no apostle and so that he himself might found churches there" (quoted from Hengel and Schwemer, *Paul between Damascus and Antioch*, p. 110).

Arabia is to be understood as the Nabatean kingdom. The boundaries of this kingdom were somewhat fluid during the Middle Nabatean period (30 B.C.–A.D. 70), but appear to have included what is today the Sinai, the Negev, the east side of the Jordan Valley rift, much of Jordan, and some of Saudi Arabia. For evidence of Jewish settlements and influence in Arabia beginning in the fourth century A.D., see E. Schürer, *The History of the Jewish People in the Age of Jesus Christ* (rev. and ed. G. Vermes, F. Millar, and M. Goodman; Edinburgh: T & T Clark, 1986), 3.1:15–17. For information on ancient historical accounts of the Nabateans and archeological remains, see A. Negev, "The Nabateans and the Province of Arabia," *ANRW* 2.8.520–686 (Berlin: de Gruyter, 1977). Hengel and Schwemer point out that the "Arab Nabateans appeared to be the closest 'kinsfolk' of the Jews who were still Gentiles" and that there was a high degree of economic, political, and cultural interchange between these neighboring territories of Nabatea and Judea (*Paul between Damascus and Antioch*, pp. 110–11).

## §5 Paul's Initial Relations with the Jerusalem Church (Gal. 1:18–24)

**1:18** / The events recounted in the next verses seem to be told in chronological order, using the same Greek adverb meaning **then** *(epeita)* at 1:18, 21; 2:1. At 1:21 and 2:1 the adverb is translated "later."

The word "then" gives the sense that only after he went away into Arabia and later returned to Damascus (v. 17) did Paul make his first post-conversion visit to Jerusalem. The stress is on the length of time, **three years,** before he went to Jerusalem. The apostle wants to make plain that when he went to Jerusalem he was not a neophyte but a person of some Christian maturity. When he went he stayed for **fifteen days.** In the ancient world, just as today, two weeks was a significant time to enjoy a host's hospitality. Paul's Jerusalem visit was a substantial one: he had one-on-one access to **Peter,** one of the most important apostles.

Paul does not describe the specifics of his visit but says its purpose was **to get acquainted.** The verb "to get acquainted" *(historēsai)* means "to inquire" (cf. 1 Esdras 1:31). It appears to be a carefully chosen word, for this is the only place it occurs in the entire NT.

**1:19** / Paul wants the Galatians to know that the contact between himself and the Jerusalem church was at his instigation and that he did not go there to be taught. The impression given is of a visit between two statesmen of equal stature who meet primarily to learn from each other.

Paul presents the beginning stage of his relationship with the Jerusalem church as respectful and limited (he **saw none of the other apostles** except **James**). He seeks to convince his Galatian readers that he was never under the authority of the Jerusalem church and that his initial relations with them were limited but cordial.

**1:20** / The following exclamation demonstrates that Paul suspects his readers will doubt his word on this—**I assure you before God that what I am writing you is no lie.** It is not unusual for Paul to have to defend his integrity (see 1 Thess. 2:5; 2 Cor. 1:23; 11:31). The issue of Paul's association with the Jerusalem church and how it affected the gospel he preached to the Galatians is at the forefront of his strained relationship with his converts.

**1:21–22** / The next thing he did, Paul says, was go to **Syria and Cilicia.** By recounting this Paul assures his hearers that even while he was generally known, he was **personally unknown to the churches of Judea that are in Christ.** The context provided by the next verse suggests that Paul identifies as being "in Christ" those churches in Judea that acknowledge his preaching. Paul can affirm as "in Christ" churches that he did not found.

**1:23–24** / In the next sentence Paul dramatizes his claim that although he had no personal contact with the churches of Judea, they nevertheless thought of his activity as cause for glorifying God: **The man who formerly persecuted us is now preaching the faith he once tried to destroy.** Paul asserts his credibility by citing what others say about him. Even those whom he has never met recognize him as one who proclaims what they too believe: "the faith." It is especially important to Paul's point to assert that he was recognized by believers in Judea, since the troublemakers claim that they have the same support. Paul's statement includes the Judean churches "in Christ" as his—not the troublemakers'—backers.

So Paul's record of events is that in the first part of his ministry he functioned on the authority of God's commission and not as a delegate of the churches of Judea; he worked in regions other than Judea; yet his work was approved of by the churches "in Christ" in Judea.

---

### Additional Notes §5

---

**1:18** / The name Peter is "Cephas" in Greek, which is the Aramaic form of Peter. The name Cephas occurs also in 2:9, 11, 14. It is found also at 1 Cor. 1:12; 3:22; 9:5; and 15:5, where it refers to a person of great eminence in the Christian community. The name Peter *(Petros)* appears in Paul's letters only at Gal. 2:7–8. Most scholars have equated Cephas with Peter. See R. E. Brown, K. P. Donfried, and J. Reumann, *Peter in the New Testament* (Minneapolis: Augsburg/New York: Paulist Press, 1973), p. 23. There is, however, a tradition going back to Clement of Alexandria's *Hypotyposeis*, recorded by Eusebius, that the Cephas referred to at Gal. 2:11 "was one of the seventy disciples" who happened to have the same name as the apostle Peter (*Ecclesiastical History* 1.12.2 [Lake, LCL]). For a sketch of the argument for understanding Cephas and Peter as two different people, see B. D. Ehrman, *The New Testament: A Historical Introduction to the Early Christian Writings* (New York: Oxford University Press, 1997), p. 288. An additional point in favor of this hypothesis is that Cephas is here mentioned before James. When the gospel tradition speaks of James and Peter it typically puts Peter first (e.g., Mark 9:2). Nevertheless, since our translation equates Cephas with Peter we will do so in the commentary.

Hengel and Schwemer also observe that fifteen days is a substantial visit (*Paul between Damascus and Antioch,* p. 149).

**1:19** / Paul describes James as **the Lord's brother** (see Mark 6:3) and as one of the apostles; in his other letters Paul mentions James only in 1 Cor. 15:7. James is an acknowledged leader of the Christian movement (see also Acts 12:17), and Paul sees him as having a powerful role in the Jerusalem church (see also 2:12). Eusebius records that James was "the first elected to the throne of the bishopric of the Church in Jerusalem" (*Ecclesiastical History* 2.1.2 [Lake, LCL]).

There are other significant men in the early Christian movement also called James: James the son of Zebedee (Mark 3:17) and James the son of Alphaeus (Mark 3:18). It is possible also that James the son of Mary (Mark 16:1) and James the father of Judas (Luke 6:16; Acts 1:13) refer to two other men bearing this name.

**1:21** / The regions of **Syria and Cilicia** refer to a fairly large area. Paul has travelled extensively.

# §6 Paul's Second Visit to the Jerusalem Church (Gal. 2:1–2)

**2:1–2** / Paul says his next visit to Jerusalem was not for another fourteen years. We do not know if the **fourteen years later** refers to fourteen years after his conversion or after his first visit to Jerusalem. Paul says he and **Barnabas** went up together and that he took Titus with him. Barnabas and Paul had a functional partnership—Paul must have trusted Barnabas to share his views, or he would not have wanted him present at the Jerusalem meeting. At this stage of his ministry Paul identifies Barnabas as his ally in evangelizing the gospel to the Gentiles (see also 2:9). His trust in Barnabas is clear in 1 Corinthians 9:6 as well. This makes the fact that Barnabas does not see the significance of Peter's behavior at Antioch (2:13) all the more distressing for Paul.

The Greek reads as if **Titus** has less seniority than Barnabas, for Paul writes that he takes Titus **along** *(symparalabōn)*. The rest of Paul's letters indicate, however, that he trusted Titus with the most delicate of tasks, such as work on the collection project (2 Cor. 8:6). The way Paul mentions Titus may also signal that the apostle intentionally took Titus, an uncircumcised Greek, along to confront the Jerusalem church leaders with the matter of uncircumcised believers. Paul's special commitment to bringing Titus is signaled in the Greek text of 2:3, which suggests that Paul did so primarily because Titus was a "Greek." By taking Titus along Paul demonstrates to the Jerusalem church his conviction that Jews and Gentiles are one in Christ. Paul may well be setting up a subtle contrast between his actions and those of Peter, which he will shortly denounce (2:11–14). Whereas in Paul's view Peter at Antioch acted hypocritically in front of the people from Jerusalem, the apostle commends himself to the Galatians as one who has the courage of his convictions.

Paul's convictions and actions stem from nothing other than a **revelation.** The Greek word used for "revelation" *(apokalypsin)* has the sense of "to uncover." It was originally used of uncovering important or vulnerable parts of the body, such as the head or chest. When the word is used metaphorically in Jewish and Christian religious contexts it suggests the uncovering of something previously hidden. Often such uncovering is understood to require God's action (e.g., 1 Cor. 2:10) or to result in disclosing things of God (Eph. 3:3–5; see Additional Notes).

By stating that his return visit to Jerusalem was by revelation Paul aligns himself with the sensibilities of his converts. He claims to have acted in response to an extraordinary religious experience, thereby communicating that his authority and his actions come from God. Prior to their conversion to Christ the Galatians' religiosity had included an awareness of the cosmos as spiritually alive (4:9). Here and elsewhere (see 3:1—"who has bewitched you?") Paul uses language familiar to his pagan readers' religious sensibilities. Pagan people understood reference to revelation as an important part of a prophet's or religious person's credibility. The gods were understood to be present and accessible to those with eyes to see; through various extraordinary means and experiences such as oracle, ecstatic visions, and dreams, human beings could gain access to divine power and knowledge.

Paul's reference to revelation works in another way to stress his independence from the Jerusalem church. He did not revisit Jerusalem in response to the mother church's request. Paul went up to Jerusalem in a position of strength, as one acting in response to divine instructions.

In this visit Paul comes as a seasoned missionary. Paul describes his task as one in which he **set before** the Jerusalem church his gospel for Gentiles. The Greek word for "set before" *(anatithēmi)* suggests that Paul took the purpose of his visit as that of seriously and thoroughly putting forth his gospel. Paul's choice of the words "set before" resonates with language used in contexts of political consultation when a cause is presented for approval or judgment. The implication is that Paul knew that he was on trial. But for Paul the gospel to the Gentiles is in accordance with God's will and so, while he is called on to defend it, there is no question about its truth. Paul at once identifies himself with the gospel he preaches and considers himself a servant of the gospel (1:15–16). His credibility is determined by the gospel, which he knows to be true. **I preach** is in the present tense, indicating that Paul has not changed his mind since the Jerusalem meeting. His gospel remains consistent.

The phrase **those who seemed to be leaders** translates a Greek construction *(hoi dokountes)* that appears twice in 2:6 and again at 2:9. In each case the NIV translates the construction differently: 2:6 has "those who seemed to be important" and then "those men"; and 2:9 has "those reputed to be." The meaning of the term is "the influential, those of reputation." While Paul may be using the term somewhat ironically, he must have had a certain degree of respect for the Jerusalem leaders, not only because of their evident influence in the communities he himself started but also because they were first in the faith (cf. 1 Cor. 15:3–11).

Paul recognizes the power the Jerusalem Christians have to nullify his own work on behalf of the gospel. They could make his efforts akin to having **run** his **race in vain,** and thus hurt the gospel, but Paul implies that this would be in disobedience to God. While Paul expresses concern that he himself could run in vain, he displays no fear that his gospel could come to naught through the actions of the Jerusalem church.

Paul, like other ancient and modern writers, is fond of athletic imagery, which he uses in describing commitment to the gospel (e.g., 1 Cor. 9:24–27). Later in this letter Paul affirms that until now the Galatians had been running well (5:7). In Philippians, using almost the same words, Paul expresses his hope that he would not have run in vain (2:16). In the Philippian letter the test will be in the "day of Christ," whereas in Galatians Paul's focus is on the meeting at Jerusalem. While the apostle does not accord the Jerusalem leaders any authority over himself or his gospel, he does recognize how significant their influence is and thus how critical is their acceptance of his gospel.

---

### Additional Notes §6

---

**2:1** / We could read the word **again** to indicate that Barnabas had been to Jerusalem before. The fact that Barnabas is readily influenced by "the men from James" (2:13) may suggest a connection with Jerusalem (so Hengel and Schwemer, *Paul between Damascus and Antioch,* p. 215). This would corroborate Luke's account of Barnabas as one involved with Jerusalem Christians (Acts 4:36–37).

**2:2** / "The Greek encounters his gods primarily in the unusual," writes A. Oepke, *"apokalyptō, apokalypsis," TDNT* 3:565.

## §7 Paul Stands Firm and the Truth of His Gospel Is Recognized (Gal. 2:3–6)

**2:3** / Proof of the truth of his gospel is that at the Jerusalem meeting **not even Titus, who was with** him, **was compelled to be circumcised, even though he was a Greek.** The word "compel" *(anagkazō)* conveys the sense that there were high stakes surrounding whether or not Titus would or should be circumcised. In light of how much pressure there was to circumcise Titus, the fact that in the end he was not circumcised reflects well on Paul's gospel. Paul emphasizes that Titus was an uncircumcised Greek so as to stress an identification between Titus and the Galatian readers—just as Titus is an uncircumcised Greek, so are they. Since Titus was not compelled to be circumcised, the Jerusalem church clearly does not consider circumcision intrinsic to faith in Christ. From this it follows that those who are troubling the Galatians by telling them that faith in Christ requires following the law are out of sync with the opinion of the leaders in Jerusalem. Paul explicitly includes the Galatians in his telling of this story when he says that the freedom that he protected at that meeting in Jerusalem was freedom that the Galatians and he now have in Christ Jesus. Paul's unswerving conviction saved the Galatians from enslavement.

**2:4–5** / While he was with the Jerusalem Christians Paul says that **false brothers . . . infiltrated.** The Greek reads as if these believers acted with the help of some in the gathering who let them in *(tous pareisaktous)* and on their own agency *(pareisēlthon).* The theme of hypocrisy is strong throughout this chapter and plays against the opposite theme of truth. Paul defends and preserves the **truth of the gospel** in the face of the falsehood of the brothers at Jerusalem and what he identifies as the hypocrisy of Peter and the rest of the Jews (2:13) at Antioch. Paul charges that at Jerusalem particular Christians (the false believers) were

allowed in for the purpose of spying on the **freedom** that they
had **in Christ Jesus.** Of course, the "false brothers" charged that
Paul was hypocritical and false. Paul defends himself against
such charges throughout the letter: he is the one who clings to
the truth of the gospel; he is the one who acts with the courage of
his convictions and sticks to his principles.

In defending himself Paul caricatures his opponents as
false. Paul also presents the goals of these "false brothers" as
seeking to **make . . . slaves** of the supporters of the Gentile mission. This, of course, would not be how the false brothers themselves understand their motives. They believed that since Jesus is
the Messiah, believers in him should be obedient Jews; this is not
bondage but a privilege. Paul, however, regards their conviction
as sinister and aggressive. He obviously feels threatened by their
actions but asserts that he and his cohorts **did not give in to them
for a moment.**

Paul wants the Galatians to know that despite the over-
whelming and intimidating opposition he experienced during
that assembly at Jerusalem, he did not allow himself to be put in
the position of a subordinate. He did this for the sake of the truth
of the gospel, so that it **might remain** for the Galatians. Paul presents himself as the real defender of the gospel.

For Paul the truth of the gospel is what he has already
given the Galatians (1:9) and what he will reiterate during the
course of the letter—that "a man is justified not by observing the
law, but by faith in Jesus Christ" (2:16). Whether Paul's presentation of the rival evangelists' position is fair or not, it is clear that
Paul was willing to go to almost any lengths to defend the
Gentiles' right to be believers in Jesus Christ without having to
adopt the Jewish law.

**2:6** / Paul is not overawed by the Jerusalem church
leaders. Paul describes the leaders as "those who seemed to be
important." Implying that whereas others might be intimidated
by their current eminence in the Jerusalem church and perhaps
their past association with Jesus, Paul writes: **whatever they
were makes no difference to me; God does not judge by external
appearance.** In a situation where the external—circumcision—is
being advocated as essential, this statement is also an implicit
criticism of his opponents' position.

Paul asserts that the influential Christian leaders, unlike
the rival evangelists, **added nothing to** his **message.** The gospel

that was preached to the Galatians came directly from God, and it was recognized as complete by the Jerusalem leaders.

## Additional Notes §7

**2:3–5** / **Even Titus:** The Greek is ambiguous. Does this phrase refer to Paul's reason for bringing Titus to the Jerusalem meeting: because he was a Greek? Or does the phrase relate to the effect of Titus' presence at the Jerusalem meeting: even though he was a Greek circumcision was not required of him?

The words **not . . . compelled to be circumcised** take on a different meaning depending on how one reads 2:5. A number of manuscripts, including one Western text and Marcion, omit the words "to them [we] did not." The reading of 2:5 in these texts is that Paul did yield to the "false brothers" with the result that Timothy was circumcised. Thus 2:3 would mean that Timothy was not compelled to be circumcised by the real leaders of the church in Jerusalem but only by the false ones. While there are other places where Paul recognizes situations in which it is appropriate to curtail one's freedom (e.g., 1 Cor. 9), he stresses that this is to be done for the sake of weaker members of the church.

At Jerusalem, as Paul presents the scenario, those who insist on circumcision are not weak but **false.** Nevertheless, it may be possible to understand the variant reading as being in sync with Paul's willingness to limit freedom for the sake of others. If we were to accept the variant reading, we might construe a situation in which the Galatians know that Titus was circumcised and in which this is being used by the rival evangelists as evidence for the Jerusalem church's stance on law observance. Paul here is putting his own spin on the incident: while Titus was circumcised this did not occur at the insistence of the leaders but rather of the false brothers. While Paul, Titus, and some others submitted to the demands of the false brothers, it was only **for a moment,** and it was for the greater good. In fact, their submission to the false brothers was sacrificial—for the sake of the gospel and future converts, **that the truth of the gospel might remain with you.** In this understanding of the event, circumcision for Titus was neither a requirement on the part of the Jerusalem leaders nor a lapse in principle on Paul's part but an acquiescence to the demand of false brothers for a greater purpose.

The variant reading of 2:5 could also be read to accord with Paul's statement in 5:11, "if I am still preaching circumcision, why am I still being persecuted?" This verse suggests that one of the pieces in the opponents' platform is that Paul is a hypocrite, telling the Galatians that they do not need to be circumcised and yet preaching or agreeing to circumcision elsewhere.

Yet despite some good reasons for seriously considering the variant reading, the majority reading, in which Paul denies that he and Barnabas and Titus yielded to the demand for Titus's circumcision, seems the most likely. Beyond the fact that most manuscripts attest to this reading, it is hard to imagine how at the same meeting James, Peter, and John could agree to the validity of a Gentile mission (2:9) and yet be party to compelling a Greek to be circumcised. Furthermore, if Paul had proven himself open to circumcising a Greek, the energetic concern of Jewish Christians to get Paul's converts to be circumcised is hard to explain.

# §8 Paul's Commission Is Acknowledged (Gal. 2:7–10)

**2:7–8** / Although Paul does not present himself as need-ing the backing or agreement of the Jerusalem leaders in order to defend his gospel, he asserts that he has this backing: these men came to see that he **had been entrusted with the task of preach-ing the gospel to the Gentiles.** The Jerusalem leaders accept his gospel and understand Paul to be in a comparable position to **Peter,** who has a gospel for **the Jews.**

Paul's claim that he was recognized as having been com-missioned with preaching the gospel to the Gentiles reads in Greek, "the gospel of the uncircumcision." This can also mean the gospel with reference to the uncircumcised. Paul's gospel is contextual, as is Peter's. Moreover, in describing his gospel this way Paul gives honor to being uncircumcised, which was a nega-tive category from the Jewish perspective. From the perspective of being "in Christ" Paul turns the category of not being circum-cised into a positive one. The gospel of the *un*circumcised is a gospel of completeness; it is a gospel to which nothing need be added.

Paul describes the meeting with the Jerusalem Christians as one in which he was recognized as a leader on a par with Peter. With this presentation Paul hopes to counter some of the negative reputation that he has been getting in Galatia and show that the Jerusalem church is in agreement with his gospel. It is those preaching a law-observant gospel to Gentiles who are at odds with Jerusalem.

Peter's influence and importance at this point in the Chris-tian movement is clear. Paul thinks he can best convey the credi-bility of his own position by putting it on a par with Peter's. Peter's mission is to the Jews, "to the circumcised"; Paul's is to the Gentiles (2:7–8). Paul goes on to assert that the leaders saw that **God, who was at work in the ministry of Peter . . . was also at**

**work in my ministry.** The decision of the Jerusalem leaders to recognize Paul's ministry was not a political or bureaucratic one but rather an acknowledgment of the activity of God. Since the most significant people in the Christian movement recognized God's work in his ministry, the Galatians should not let themselves be swayed by the rival evangelists' deprecation of his gospel.

Paul refers to his apostleship as "to the Gentiles" (v. 8). This is a literal rendering of the Greek and functions in parallel with "to the circumcised" of verse 7. While Paul continues to refer to Peter's gospel and apostleship as for "the circumcised," Paul changes the description of his own mission field from that of "the uncircumcised" to "the Gentiles." This indicates perhaps that when recounting the incident at Jerusalem, he begins from the categories established by the opponents—circumcision versus uncircumcision. But as Paul continues his presentation he demonstrates that he primarily understands his role to be preaching the gospel to the Gentiles, to those who are the nations, the ones for whom God's promise to Abraham was extended from the beginning. This accords with the apostle's description of his call and commission in 1:15–16; the people to whom he is to preach the gospel are "the Gentiles/nations." Paul's gravitation to using the word "Gentiles" strongly suggests that the issue of circumcision versus uncircumcision came from those opposed to Paul's law-free gospel. For Paul the gospel that was revealed to him was beyond the categories of circumcision and uncircumcision (6:15).

Paul says that God worked through Peter for the purpose of making him an apostle to the Jews, or the circumcised. He does not refer to himself as an apostle in this context, perhaps because he has already stressed this point (1:1) and because his certainty of his own apostleship allows Paul to recognize Peter as an apostle also.

**2:9** / For Paul it is God who is the source of his and Peter's ministry. In the Greek there is a parallel between verse 9 and verse 7. In verse 7 the leaders see God's work through Paul, and in verse 9 they **recognized** God's work (this same word "work" occurs twice in v. 8). By the end of his time with the important Jerusalem church leaders Paul had convinced them of the validity of his gospel. As a result of their recognizing **the grace** that had been **given** to Paul, James and Peter and John **gave the right hand of fellowship** to Paul **and Barnabas.** Paul's explicit mention of his acceptance by the three most prominent leaders in the church of the time serves further to validate his own position. Early Christian tradition generally connected Peter, James, and John (e.g., Mark 9:2). Their direct link with Jesus accounted in large measure for their unparalleled authority within the early church.

**James** is mentioned first in the list. He is featured also in 2:12, where he is presented as one whose authority intimidates even Peter, and 1:19, where he is described as the brother of the Lord. Paul's atypically plentiful references to James in this letter (the only other time he mentions James is 1 Cor. 15:7) and his mentioning James first suggest that subsequent to Paul's leaving Galatia his converts have come to regard James as the most important leader of the faith. This is the only place in his letters where Paul mentions **John,** who is usually understood to be the disciple John the son of Zebedee (Mark 3:17).

**2:10** / The only thing that the Jerusalem church required of Paul and Barnabas was that they should **remember the poor.** The tense and mood of the Greek verb *mnēmoneuōmen,* translated "remember," conveys the sense of continuing action and could denote either that Paul was already remembering the poor and is encouraged to continue to do so or that he is directed now continually to remember the poor. The context would suggest the former meaning. Just as the church affirmed his gospel so they encourage him to continue to do what he is already doing—remembering the poor. Paul's expression is not the expression of one **eager** to please but an affirmation that he wishes to continue to do the same thing to which he is already committed. Paul's point is that he is not under the Jerusalem church's authority; rather, he is an equal partner in the gospel.

It seems to be the case that "the poor" refers to the Jerusalem Christians (see Additional Notes). Thus this request to remember the poor further emphasizes Paul's good standing with the Jerusalem church. By the end of his meeting the divine authentication of his gospel had been recognized and the Jerusalem believers were willing to remain in a position of some dependence upon him, since they would expect him to bring financial aid from the Gentile churches. There could not be a much greater sign that the mother church had fully accepted his ministry. The fact of the collection indicates that there was at this stage a high degree of unity between the churches of Paul and the leadership in Jerusalem.

## Additional Notes §8

**2:10** / Reference to **the poor** is most likely to Jerusalem Jewish Christians. Paul here as elsewhere (Rom. 15:26) refers to the situation of inhabitants of Jerusalem. The economic conditions of all Jerusalem dwellers were affected by the existence of a significant number of beggars. J. Jeremias notes that

> When tradition talks of "proud poverty" in Jerusalem (b. Pes. 113a), it gives unwarranted praise, for Jerusalem in the time of Jesus was already a centre of mendiancy; it was encouraged because alms-giving was regarded as particularly meritorious when done in the Holy City. . . . Jerusalem had already in Jesus' time become a city of idlers, and the considerable proletariat living on the religious importance of the city was one of its most outstanding peculiarities (*Jerusalem in the Time of Jesus* [trans. F. H. Cave and C. H. Cave; London: SCM, 1969], pp. 116, 118)

Believers in Christ may also have had their own particular reasons for being poor: the principle of communal sharing (Acts 4:32–37), people who had left job and family to join the movement, persecution, etc. On the reasons for and meaning of the collection, see B. Holmberg, *Paul and Power: The Structure of Authority in the Primitive Church as Reflected in the Pauline Epistles* (Philadelphia: Fortress, 1978), pp. 35–43.

Reference to "the poor" may also be a meritorious self-designation such as is found in the Qumran scrolls, in which poverty was an ideal that signified piety and purity. For instance, in the *War Scroll* we find the prophecy that God will "deliver into the hands of the poor the enemies from all the lands, to humble the mighty of the peoples by the hand of those bent to the dust" (11.9–13; quoted from G. Vermes, *The Dead Sea Scrolls in English* [New York: Penguin, 1984], p. 117). See also *Commentary on Habakkuk* 12.3, 6, 10; *Rule of the Blessings* 5.21. The Jerusalem Jewish Christians may have been appropriating for themselves such a connection between poverty and holiness. There is evidence elsewhere within Jewish Christianity for regarding the poor as those who are closest to the kingdom of God (Jas. 2:5). And in speaking of his collection project (see Rom. 15:25–27; 1 Cor. 16:1–4), Paul refers to those in Jerusalem for whom he is collecting funds both as saints and as the poor (Rom. 15:26).

For a discussion of the collection as indication of unity between Paul and the Jerusalem leaders, see Hill, *Hellenists and Hebrews*, pp. 174, 178.

## §9 Paul's Presentation of His Confrontation with Peter at Antioch (Gal. 2:11–13)

**2:11** / Paul continues to present his relationship with the Jerusalem Christians to the Galatians. In the next verses he recounts an incident with **Peter** that occurred at **Antioch.** It is almost certain that the Galatians had already heard of this incident, for before describing it Paul declares the sides in the case (Paul **opposed** Peter **to his face**) and pronounces the verdict (Peter **was in the wrong**). But it seems that the Galatians have understood this incident from a different perspective—one in which Peter, not Paul, is the hero.

If later church tradition is correct regarding Peter as the first bishop of the church at Antioch, Paul's presentation of the incident becomes all the more impressive. Paul claims that at Antioch he demonstrated that Peter—the most eminent Christian—was in the wrong. The Greek participial construction translated "in the wrong" *(kategnōsmenos ēn)* expresses Paul's perception that Peter had been "in the wrong" over a period of time but that when Paul opposed him Peter discontinued his actions. Consequently Peter is now not condemned. Paul may be using this story in part to counter any rumors that he and Peter remain at odds after the incident. The record follows naturally from Paul's record of his triumph at the Jerusalem meeting: at Jerusalem Peter and Paul are recognized as partners in the gospel; at Antioch Paul's law-free gospel is accepted by Peter.

**2:12** / Paul says that **before certain men came from James,** it was Peter's practice **to eat with the Gentiles.** According to Paul, Peter changed his behavior not on principle or in line with the faith but **because he was afraid.** Paul portrays Peter in this incident as one who **draw[s] back** out of fear and who therefore exhibits his "hypocrisy." Paul's presentation of Peter implicitly reflects well on himself, since Paul is unafraid, even in the face of the most significant people from the Jerusalem church.

One function of this story is to acknowledge the difficulties of a situation in which, even though there was an agreement at Jerusalem (2:1–10), people from Jerusalem who did not accept the law-free gospel for Gentiles have a continuing and formidable influence, even over the likes of the apostle Peter. The "men from James" are a fearsome group. By recounting this story Paul lets the Galatian readers know that their experience of being persuaded by the rival evangelists is neither unprecedented nor shameful.

Throughout this section Paul has been making a distinction between the Jews/circumcised and the Gentiles/uncircumcised. His reference here is framed slightly differently. The Greek reads literally "those of the circumcision," and the parallelism in the verse makes it clear that the circumcision group is the same as "certain men . . . from James." Perhaps this is the same group of people who let the false believers into the Jerusalem meeting and who, despite the agreement of James, Peter, and John to Paul's gospel (2:9), remained convinced of the rightness of law-observant Gentile Christianity.

If we can trust early church tradition that Peter was the founder of the church at Antioch, then the statement in Galatians 2:12—along with the corroborative evidence in Acts that Peter recognized that the gospel was for Gentiles (Acts 10:1–11:18)—suggests that Peter established a church in which Jewish and Gentile believers saw themselves as a single social unit. The fact that subsequently Peter could be influenced by those promoting separation indicates the degree of social pressure that fell on a new religious movement that did not fit within the Jewish or the pagan ethos. A religion that embraced Jews and non-Jews, requiring only faith in Christ, faced the daunting task of creating a new social space for itself.

The Greek for the verb **to eat** *(synesthiō)* is in a progressive tense, which suggests that it was over a period of time that Peter joined Gentiles for meals. There are several reasons to understand the meals Peter was eating as ordinary as opposed to eucharistic meals. First, whereas in other places Paul clearly refers to the Lord's Supper (1 Cor. 11:20–21), here he does not. Secondly, given that Paul elsewhere connects eating the Lord's Supper with the principle of social harmony among the participants (1 Cor. 11:17–34), we may assume that if the meals at Antioch had been eucharistic he would have appealed to this principle in service of his position. Furthermore, on the presumption that if Paul does not mention the Lord's Supper we should understand his references to eating are to ordinary meals, we have corroborative evidence in Romans (ch. 14) for Jewish and Gentile believers eating ordinary meals communally, or at least for Christian Jews and Gentiles having close enough social contact that they knew what each other ate.

The translation **circumcision group** conveys the sense that these men from James were on a circumcising campaign. While we know that Paul is concerned about such people in Galatia (6:12), it is far from clear that his opponents in Antioch were preaching circumcision. In the Greek the phrase means simply "those of the circumcision," that is, Jews. Read in the context of the preceding passage, in which the circumcision refers to the Jews (2:7), verse 12 most likely indicates the ethnic identity of the men from James. Paul's clarification that these men were Jews draws the Galatians' attention to the investment in being respected by his kinsfolk held by Peter, the apostle to the Jews.

The dynamics of hypocrisy and truth play loudly in these verses. Paul has no doubt but that he is on the side of truth. Paul charges that Peter's change of behavior when the visitors from Jerusalem came was not "in line with the truth of the gospel" (v. 14). Until the arrival of the "men from James" the Jewish Peter had, on account of the gospel, lived "like a Gentile and not like a Jew." With the arrival of the Jerusalem contingent, however, Peter separated himself from his Gentile brothers and sisters in Christ and adopted the stance of the "circumcision group"—a stance that would "force Gentiles to follow Jewish customs." Paul's charge is that this is contrary to Peter's previous practice, in which he had demonstrated his understanding that there is no distinction between Gentile and Jew in Christ.

**2:13** / Peter and those who followed his lead changed their direction out of hypocrisy and fear. Paul's comment that **even Barnabas** was swayed by Peter's response to the Jerusalem Christians may give the Galatians a means of retreating in a dignified fashion from the position they have now put themselves in. The fact that even Barnabas—who along with Paul had convinced the Jerusalem Christians of the validity of Gentile Christianity—could be led astray makes the Galatians' temptation to follow the rival evangelists at least understandable.

Paul makes clear that Peter changes his behavior in response to "the circumcision group" rather than to the "men from James." This suggests that the circumcision group was a smaller subgroup of the "men from James." Just as there was dissension over Paul's gospel at the meeting in Jerusalem between "some false brothers" and the church's leaders, so it may be that the visitors from Jerusalem display discord among themselves when they visit Antioch.

Paul's mention of **other Jews** who join in Peter's response to the people from James gives evidence that the congregation at Antioch had a significant number of Jewish Christians; that initially these Jewish Christians had felt comfortable with close interaction with Gentile Christians; and that Peter had played a leadership role among Jewish Christians at Antioch.

### Additional Notes §9

For a detailed exegesis of Gal. 2:11–18 that includes analysis of Jewish texts regarding table fellowship, see Dunn, "The Incident at Antioch, pp. 129–82.

**2:11** / Theoretically there are two possible geographical references for **Antioch:** either Antioch in Syria or Antioch in Pisidia. Pisidian Antioch was geographically closer to the addressees and so the Galatians would have had more reason to be interested in what occurred there. Yet almost all Pauline scholars understand him to be referring to the more distant Syrian Antioch. There is strong church tradition regarding Peter's influence at Antioch in Syria. Eusebius, referring to Syrian Antioch, writes that Ignatius was "the second after Peter to succeed to the bishopric of Antioch" (*Ecclesiastical History* 3.36.2 [Lake, LCL]). Paul's account gives evidence that Peter and others from the Jerusalem church took a strong interest in the Antiochene Christian congregation. In light of later church tradition that connects Peter with Syrian Antioch, Paul's reference to Antioch is most probably to that in Syria.

Along with Rome and Alexandria, Syrian Antioch was one of the major cities of the Greco-Roman world, drawing commercial and political visitors from all over that world. The Christian community at Antioch included a number of Jews, as 2:13 indicates. The Jewish population in Syrian Antioch was large, perhaps because it was such a politically and economically strategic city and perhaps also because this city, being under Roman government, offered Diaspora Jews the protection of Roman law. Josephus describes the relations between Greeks and Jews at Antioch as fairly harmonious (*War* 7.44) and says that the Jews were constantly "attracting to their worship a great number of Greeks"

(*War* 7.45; trans. Williamson). He mentions also that during the war Jews were spared only in Antioch, Sidon, and Apamea (*War* 2.479). Yet the sixth-century chronicler Malalas records that in A.D. 40 the Jews of Antioch were attacked and many killed by the pagan residents, who also burned their synagogues. G. Downey suggests that among the reasons for the pogrom may have been the preaching of Christianity (*A History of Antioch in Syria from Seleucus to the Arab Conquest* [Princeton: Princeton University Press, 1961], p. 194). If Malalas's record is historically credible it helps to explain why the circumcision group might have been concerned to keep the church within the bounds of Judaism. If there was friction between Jew and Gentile in Antioch at this time, from their point of view fragmentation within the Jewish community could only lead to more tensions. A group of people with feet in both Jewish and non-Jewish circles (i.e., Gentile Christians) would unsettle further an already tenuous host environment for the Jewish community.

**2:12** / O. Cullmann is correct in describing Peter's understanding of the gospel as very close to Paul's (*Peter: Disciple, Apostle, Martyr: A Historical and Theological Study* [trans. F. V. Filson; 2d ed.; {London: SCM, 1962}, p. 66]).

There are some parallels between the Galatian situation and the story of the circumcision of Izates, in which Izates is convinced to become a full proselyte by the strong argument of Eleazar (Josephus, *Ant.* 20.17–96 [noted by J. M. G. Barclay, *Obeying the Truth: A Study of Paul's Ethics in Galatians* (Edinburgh: T & T Clark, 1988), pp. 55–56]). The significance of the food laws to Jews is made clear in the story of Eleazar, who who would rather face death than even pretend to disobey these laws (2 Macc. 6:21, 24; 4 Macc. 6:15, 17). Yet while many Jewish texts command dietary restrictions, few enjoin Jews to avoid eating with Gentiles. *Jub.* 22:16 is the one exception, and this anomaly may be the result of its provenance in a sectarian environment. E. P. Sanders notes that there are Jewish texts, such as the *Letter of Aristeas*, that display comfort with Gentiles and Jews eating together ("Jewish Association with Gentiles and Galatians 2:11–14," in *Studies in Paul and John: In Honor of J. L. Martyn* [ed. R. T. Forna and B. R. Gaventa; Nashville: Abingdon, 1990], pp. 170–88, esp. p. 178). Sanders and others point out that in the Diaspora there is evidence for Jewish involvement in civic life and therefore for social interaction between Jew and Gentile.

Scholarship on this passage often equates dietary purity with segregation from Gentiles on the presumption that this was both what Torah required and how Jews enacted the law. That is, scholars often presume that Jews in general considered following the food laws and eating separately from Gentiles as the same thing. However, there is no law requiring Jews to eat only with other Jews. Moreover, those traditions regulating what to do with food touched by Gentiles, for instance in *Avodah Zarah*, give evidence that Jews might eat in close proximity to Gentiles while keeping their dietary laws. The Mishnah's prescriptions about how to maintain the law when in contact with Gentiles and/or Gentile food (e.g., *Eruvin* 6:1) are evidence that Jews did not isolate themselves. For one thing, the population density of the ancient city and the closeness of village life would have made social contact inevitable between Jew and Gentile. It was possible in the first century to be both an observant Jew and occasionally to share a table with Gentiles.

There was, however, one Jewish group that allowed for casual contact with Gentiles but that required meals to be eaten separately from the uncircumcised. The Pharisees, whom J. Neusner dubs a "table-fellowship group" (*From Politics to Piety: The Emergence of Pharisaic Judaism* [Englewood Cliffs, N.J.: Prentice-Hall, 1973], p. 80), advocated eating everyday meals in ritual purity. Unlike the Essenes, the Pharisees remained part of urban life, but they still separated themselves from Gentiles at meals. The "circumcision group" appears to have been influenced by this branch of first-century Judaism.

## §10 Paul's Record of His Conversation with Peter (Gal. 2:14–17)

**2:14** / Paul records that he challenged Peter by saying **"You are a Jew, yet you live like a Gentile and not like a Jew. How is it, then, that you force Gentiles to follow Jewish customs?"** In the Greek construction the first clause is an "if clause" ("If you, though a Jew"), and Paul's challenge works on the basis that the "if clause" is true. The resulting question is, how then does it make sense for Peter to compel Gentiles to live in a Jewish manner? It is a curious retort, since from the way that Paul recounts the Antioch incident it appears as if the issue was that Peter was expecting Jews to live in a Jewish manner. It is likely that Paul styles the retort he gave at Antioch so that it fits the Galatian situation, in which Gentiles are being compelled to live like Jews. As Paul presents his confrontation with Peter he continues to play on the theme of Peter's hypocrisy, underscoring that Gentiles cannot be required to adopt Jewish practice on the basis of Peter's actions or authority. The same Greek word translated "force" (*anankazeis*) is used here and in 2:3, where Paul describes how Titus was not "compelled [or forced] to be circumcised" at Jerusalem, even though Peter was there. This repetition of the word brings home Peter's hypocrisy: at one point he agreed that it was acceptable to commune with Gentiles, but at Antioch, perhaps under the influence of the same group who helped the false believers to sneak into the Jersualem meeting (2:4), Peter is willing to reverse his position and compel Gentiles to live like Jews.

The Greek verb *orthopodousin*, translated in the phrase **not acting in line**, gives the impression that Paul was willing to allow some room for error to those who had not had such a direct revelation of the truth of the gospel as he had been privileged with, as long as they were heading on the right course. But Paul considers that by their actions at Antioch Peter and the others got off the road that leads toward the truth. Consequently when Paul saw this he challenged Peter **in front of them all.** Thus Paul was the courageous defender of truth in a situation comparable to the one in which the Galatians find themselves.

**2:15–16** / Before their conversion the Galatians were pagans, so when Paul writes **we who are Jews** he is obviously referring to himself and the Jewish Christians he addressed at Antioch. This suggests that verse 15 is part of Paul's record of his words to Peter. Rehearsing what Peter had come to know and believe—that a person is **not justified by observing the law, but by faith in Jesus Christ**—Paul exposes more clearly the fact that Peter acts contrary to his convictions. Paul reminds Peter that he and others **have put** their **faith in Christ Jesus that** they **may be justified by faith in Christ.** Given that Peter, like Paul, is a Jew **by birth,** such faith is all the more remarkable. Peter's Jewish background would have emphasized the centrality and nonnegotiability of the law for justification. Thus when Peter accepted the "truth of the gospel" and began to live "like a Gentile and not like a Jew," he, like Paul, had made a significant break with his Jewish roots. After faith in Christ he recognized that observing the law did not make one righteous. Paul's statement in verses 15–16 emphasizes that if even he and other Jews have come to know that a person is not justified through the law but rather through faith in Christ, then Gentiles, such as the Galatians, should not be tempted to follow law.

By underscoring that Peter and the others are born Jews, Paul distinguishes between their Jewish ethnicity and their new "in Christ" religious identity and foreshadows what will be a major theme in his letter. While Paul's adversaries may try to discredit his law-free gospel as the product of a misguided traitor, Paul asserts that his gospel is in line with God's promises and revelation to the Jewish people (see 3:6–20). As always, God's revelation comes to the Jews first. Paul and some other Jewish Christians know that justification comes from faith in Christ and not from observing the law. To bolster his point and underscore the continuity of his gospel with Judaism Paul uses a scriptural quotation—**no one will be justified** (Ps. 143:2).

Paul chooses to refer to non-Jews as **Gentile sinners** rather than as Gentiles, his more customary term. He is likely trying to unmask the mistaken presuppositions of the Jewish Christians: that for believers the distinction between Jew and Gentile remains.

The Jewish world regularly referred to non-Jews, who were without the law, as "sinners." For instance, the author of the Jewish apocalyptic book *Jubilees* speaks of "the sinners, the gentiles" (23:24; see also 1 Sam. 15:18; 1 Macc. 1:34; Tobit 13:6; *Psalms of Solomon* 1:1; 2:1). As the psalm says, the blessed person is one whose "delight is in the law of the Lord" (Ps. 1:2). In Jewish writings contemporary with Paul the effectiveness of the law for producing virtue was contrasted favorably with Greek philosophy. Philo, while recognizing that virtue was to be found in all peoples, extolls the life of the Jewish group known as the Essenes, who dedicated themselves to rigorous observance of the Jewish law. He calls them "athletes of virtue produced by a philosophy free from the pedantry of Greek wordiness" (*Good Person* 88 [Colson, LCL]).

The phrase "faith in Christ" occurs three times in verse 16. It has been argued that Paul is not really repeating himself, and that the first and third instance of this phrase refer to the faithfulness of Christ and the second instance refers to the faith of the believer (see Introduction). The Greek phrases *pisteōs Iēsou Christou* in the first instance and *pisteōs Christou* in the third may be rendered as subjective genitives. Verse 16 would then read: "knowing that a person is justified not through works of the law but through Jesus Christ's faith. And we have come to believe in Christ Jesus, so that we might be justified by Christ's faith, and not by doing the works of the law."

The Greek word translated "justified" (*dikaioutai*) is the verb from the same root as the noun "righteousness," a noun that is also translated at times as "justice." Righteousness was the goal of Jewish religion. As Deuteronomy 16:20 says, "Follow justice (*dikaiosynē*) and justice alone." The Jewish faith held that God's character is righteous and the point of observing the law was to begin to take on the character of God—righteousness. Paul was convinced that in Christ God had revealed God's righteousness in an unprecedented way (Rom. 1:17; 3:21). The consequence of the death and resurrection of Jesus is that the "righteousness of God" is now available to those who have faith in Jesus Christ and are "in Christ."

Righteousness, or justice, was also a concern of ancient Greek philosophers. Plato's *Republic* deals extensively with the issue of justice. Aristotle regards justice, along with courage, as the most important virtue (*Rhetoric* 1.9.1366b). Plutarch regards justice as the most enviable virtue, saying that "the common folk . . . do not merely honour the just . . . they actually love the just, and put confidence and trust in them" (*Cato the Younger* 44.8 [Perrin, LCL]). To be just was to be like a god (Plutarch, *Aristeides* 6.2).

The battle between Paul and his opponents, then, was over convincing the Galatians not of the desirability of righteousness but of the correct means of becoming righteous. The hook that the rival evangelists had in the Galatians was that their way—the way of works of law—resonated both with the Jewish tradition to which Paul's converts were attracted and with the Greek philosophical tradition that thought virtue was achieved through human agency (e.g., Aristotle, *Eth. nic.* 3.3.13).

The final phrase of verse 16 reads literally "by works of law all **flesh** (*sarx*) will not be justified." Flesh for Paul has several different meanings. It refers to bodily existence, in which case it has a neutral, straightforward meaning (4:13–14). It also has theological meaning. The "flesh" is not justified (2:16) but is capable of being transformed through faith (2:20 reads lit. "the life I now live in the flesh"). Flesh is opposed to Spirit (3:3; 5:16) and remains a dynamic in the Christian life—a force that tempts the believer to serve its needs rather than God and the needs of others (5:13, 16).

**2:17** / There is some question whether verse 17 should be read as a question Paul is now putting to his Galatian hearers or as a question he asked of Peter at Antioch. The continued use of **we** suggests that Paul is still recounting what he said to Peter at Antioch. If this is so then the **absolutely not!** at the end of the verse would be Peter's exclamation as he comes to grips with the theological consequence of separating himself from Gentiles believers.

The Jewish Christian opponents of Paul's law-free gospel work with the presupposition that the only remedy for sin is the law. To be without the law is to be a sinner. Paul's response in verse 17, which is clarified in verse 21, is that for these Jewish Christians to place their trust in the law is to reject the work of Christ, for "if righteousness could be gained through the law, Christ died for nothing." To regard the law as necessary for dealing with sin is to think that **Christ promotes sin.** If the law is added to the gospel, the logical conclusion would be that Christ is inadequate to deal with sin and that a Christ-centered, law-free gospel promotes sin.

For Paul it is either Christ or the law: there can be no compromise. As he says later, "if you let yourselves be circumcised,

Christ will be of no value to you" (5:2); and "you who are trying to be justified by law have been alienated from Christ; you have fallen away from grace" (5:4). To rely on the law to curb sin and attain righteousness is to reject Christ. Such a result is, Paul hopes, unthinkable for his Galatian readers, and so when he records Peter's emphatic "absolutely not," Paul expects that his readers will join with him in discarding the preposterous idea that Christ promotes sin. Paul hopes that through this demonstration he may dispel the influence of the rival evangelists.

Paul's choice of the words **seek to be** justified in Christ may be more than descriptive. He appears also to be making a value judgment—striving is antithetical to what it means to be in Christ. Paul uses a type of "if" clause that indicates that his readers are in fact striving for justification in Christ. He criticizes their framework (giving credence to law) and their method (effort).

---

### Additional Notes §10

---

**2:14** / The words **follow Jewish customs** translate a Gk. adverb *(Ioudaikōs)* that means "to live Jewishly." It occurs only here in the NT. In the OT it can be found at Esth. 8:17, where it speaks of acting in a Jewish manner in a context where such behavior is motivated by fear.

On becoming full proselytes through circumcision, see K. G. Kuhn, *"prosēlytos,"* TDNT 6:727–44, esp. p. 731.

**2:15–16** / Many commentators understand 2:15 to be part of Paul's address to Peter (see W. Schmithals, *Paul and James* [trans. D. M. Barton; London: SCM, 1965], pp. 72–73).

An alternative reading of 2:15–16a is: "we who are born Jews and not Gentile sinners know that a person is not made righteous through works of law unless such are done in accordance with the faithfulness of Jesus Christ (to the law)." This reading relies on two translation decisions: translating *pistis Christou* as a subjective genitive and translating *ean mē* as exceptive. Such a reading has Paul saying that Jewish believers in Jesus, such as himself and Peter, know that the only acceptable kind of law observance is that evidenced by Jesus. This viewpoint was expressed most effectively in the generation after Paul (perhaps also as a result of the Antiochene situation) by the Gospel of Matthew. In Matthew we see reflected a Jewish Christian community committed to keeping Torah because it understood Jesus as the one who correctly interpreted the law (see A. Saldarini, "The Gospel of Matthew and Jewish-Christian Conflict," in *Social History of the Matthean Community: Cross-Disciplinary Approaches* [ed. D. L. Balch; Minneapolis: Fortress, 1991], pp. 41–42). For the Matthean community and other Jewish Christians with whom Paul might agree to disagree, the law is to be kept in accordance with Jesus' interpretation. For instance, in Matthew Jesus is presented as the correct interpreter of the law who nonetheless includes Gentiles without circumcision. The Jewish Christianity that Paul can work alongside, and to which he wants to call Peter back, is one that considers Jesus' law observance as a demonstration of a new way of being holy.

Paul's position is somewhat different from what he affirms in 2:15–16a. He clarifies his own understanding in the rest of Gal. 2: Paul considers that it is through participation in Christ's faithfulness and Christ's death that a believer, whether Jew or Gentile, becomes righteous as Christ is righteous. Therefore, for Paul the law is no longer in effect as a means of righteousness.

**No one will be justified** is a quote from Ps. 143:2. Paul did not quote Scripture in all of his letters. The bulk of his scriptural quotations are in Galatians, Romans, and 1 and 2 Corinthians. It is likely that he used Scripture in his evangelistic preaching. Romans, which contains forty-five scriptural quotations, may be read as an example of Paul's missionary preaching; see L. Ann Jervis, *The Purpose of Romans: A Comparative Letter Structure Investigation* (Sheffield: Sheffield Academic Press, 1991). The apostle also used Scripture when he felt compelled to respond to his opponents' own use of Scripture. For example, the reference to Abraham in Galatians is almost certainly a rebuttal of the rival evangelists' use of the story.

On the righteousness of God and its connection with believers' faith, see Jervis, "Becoming Like God through Christ."

## §11 Paul's Continuing Defense of His Gospel in the Face of Peter's Hypocrisy (Gal. 2:18–21)

**2:18–21** / Paul continues to argue with Peter by pointing out that adding the law to the gospel would be to go backward, to rebuild what has already been destroyed and so to admit that one was mistaken all along. If Paul were now to adopt the law it would effectively **prove that** he was **a lawbreaker** when he believed in Christ as the means of justification. Paul reasons that rather than becoming a "lawbreaker" he has become one able to **live for God.** He has not broken the law but rather **died to the law,** and **through the law** itself Paul was able to die to the law. He explains this new condition by saying that he has been **crucified with Christ.**

Paul's shift to the first person may be for rhetorical purposes, in order to bring home the force of his argument by encouraging his readers to identify personally with the consequences of their view. The shift may also indicate that Paul is responding to the charge that he had advocated the law at one point but has now changed his mind. Note that the words **what I destroyed** may be read in parallelism to those in verse 19, "for through the law I died to the law." At other places in the letter Paul seems to be defending himself against such an allegation (e.g., 1:10; 5:11). In each place Paul denies this charge.

In the context of verse 18, in which Paul appears to be responding to the accusation that he is rebuilding the Judaism that he once tore down, the law refers to the whole Jewish way of life. Paul died to the Jewish way of life through two aspects of Jewish law. First, Paul's zeal for the traditions of his fathers (1:14) was in some way a preparation for God's choice of him (1:15). So by means of devotion to the law he came to die to the law. And second, Christ's death, in which Paul shares and which is now the key to righteousness, was through the law. Later in the letter Paul directly connects Christ's death with the demands of the law

(3:13). By being crucified with Christ Paul shares in the circumstances and consequences of Christ's death, which are through the law dying to the law.

Being "crucified with Christ" is a central feature of Paul's understanding of the meaning of the Christian life. The believer becomes conformed to Christ and Christ's death. Paul makes his meaning especially plain in verse 20, where he juxtaposes "I" with "Christ." In the first clause he states that he no longer lives and in the second that it is Christ who now lives in him.

For Paul the power of the Christian life resides not in intellectual assent to truth, nor in personal rigor, nor even in the simple power of confidence in God, but in recognizing that one has become incorporated into Christ. The Christian life is one of conformity with Christ. Paul uses the Greek aorist (past) tense when he says that he died to the law and the Greek perfect tense (which indicates that an event in the past has continuing results in the present) when he says he has been crucified with Christ. This suggests that Paul thought of his death to the law as having happened in the past, but he defines his life in the present as one of being crucified with Christ. This is why Paul can say **I no longer live, but Christ lives in me. The life I live in the body, I live by faith in the Son of God, who loved me and gave himself for me.** At the start of his letter Paul connects Christ's self-sacrifice with overcoming sin and rescuing believers from the present evil age (1:4). Now Paul connects the sacrifice of Christ with the believers' conformity with Christ, which involves sharing in Christ's crucifixion.

The idea of sharing in Christ's death is a central one that Paul uses to describe the type of religious life he has experienced and seeks to convey. For Paul, belief in Jesus Christ entails identifying with Christ's death and resurrection. As noted in the Introduction, when Paul refers to the faith of Christ he is speaking of the type of human life Jesus lived and in which believers too may partake. Believers do not dedicate themselves to an example but are incorporated into the archetypal human being. Paul speaks most often of the believer in Christ participating in Christ's death and resurrection. In Romans and Galatians, in particular, Paul speaks of believers conforming to Jesus' death (see esp. Rom. 6; 8). For Paul the Christian life is one of conformity to Christ, of being "in Christ," of "dying with Christ" and so being raised with Christ.

Paul's connection in verse 20 of the idea of Christ's death with the idea of being "in Christ" is consonant with his statements elsewhere (e.g., Rom. 3:24–25; 8:1–4). Scholars have often thought of Paul's "in Christ" language as mystical and seen this as a separate and sometimes antithetical theological approach from his juridical interpretation of the meaning of Christ's death, in which Christ's death is thought to atone for humanity's sin and allow believers to be righteous in God's sight. Yet here as elsewhere, Paul combines the idea of Christ living in the believer with reference to Christ's death. This suggests that Paul's understanding of the meaning of Christ's death was both a juridical and a mystical one. Paul could write about righteousness, the word that has typically been associated with a juridical understanding of Christ's death, and in the same breath he could refer to being in Christ. So Paul writes in 2 Corinthians 5:21: "God made him who had no sin to be sin, so that in him we might become the righteousness of God." In Galatians 2:16, when Paul speaks of Christ's death he refers to what has been called its "mystical" result instead of its juridical consequences.

Paul's understanding of the consequences of Christ's death cannot then be easily compartmentalized. Even to characterize part of his understanding as mystical requires qualification. Unlike ancient mystical understandings, which regarded the body as a grave for the soul and so looked forward to the separation of body and soul in order that the soul might achieve union with the incorporeal God, Paul speaks of the whole being of believers, including their "body," as being vitally affected by faith in Christ's death and resurrection (cf. Rom. 8:11).

Paul maintains a dialectic between the historical fact of the death of Christ, "who *loved* me and *gave himself* for me," and the personal appropriation of that fact ("who loved *me* and gave himself *for me*"; also "I have been crucified with Christ").

Paul typically speaks of the idea of conformity with Christ by speaking of being "in Christ" (e.g., 1:22; 2:4; 3:14, 26, 28; 5:6, 10). It is unusual for him to speak of Christ being "in him." But in verse 20 he may be saying what he said in 2:16—that faith in Christ results in justification through sharing the faith of Christ (see Introduction). That is, justification is being as Christ is, having the same faith that Christ has, which occurs because Christ lives in the believer.

"By faith" *(en pistei)* reads literally in Greek "in faith." This phrase resonates with "in Christ" and also with Paul's statement in 1:16 that God "revealed his Son in me." If a subjective genitive reading of 2:16 be accepted, thereby giving the sense of Christ's faith as that in which believers participate through their faith (see Introduction), then in 2:20 Paul would be saying that his life in the flesh is life lived in the faith of the Son of God. The quality of Paul's life of faith is that of Jesus Christ—it is Christ's faith in which Paul lives. The demonstration of that faith is that Christ loved Paul and gave himself for him. These actions are the actions of faith. And in them Paul now lives.

**Righteousness** translates the same Greek word as "justification" *(dikaiosynē)*. Paul asserts that through the death of Christ God's righteousness is now available for those who believe, and he will go on to claim that since Christ's death the law's role of guiding toward righteousness has ceased. Therefore, the problem is not that Paul is setting aside the grace of God by disregarding the law as a means to righteousness. Rather, the problem is that the rival evangelists do not understand that the grace of God is now manifested in the death of Christ. Faith in Christ allows one to be joined to Christ, to live in Christ, and to have Christ live in oneself—to be as Christ and so to live out of the same faithfulness as Christ. This is righteousness.

The role of Christ's death is to deal with sin. The role of faith in Christ is to be able to share in Christ's death and resurrection and furthermore to live with a faith that is similar to Christ's. It may be significant that in 2:20, when speaking of identification with Christ through faith, Paul refers to Christ as "the Son of God," exactly the phrase that Paul later uses to describe the identity of those who have believed in Christ Jesus. At 3:26 he writes, "you are all sons of God through faith in Christ Jesus."

The switch Paul made to the first person at verse 18 continues until the end of chapter 2. In the verses in which Paul is most personal (2:18–21) he vividly describes identification with Christ: his co-crucifixion with Christ, and the fact that Christ, not Paul, is living in Paul's body. The use of the first person makes explicit Paul's own faith convictions and highlights that for Paul, individual believers become incorporated into Christ. This results in a unity of believers in Christ and so is diametrically opposed to the rival evangelists' contention that there should be a division between circumcised and uncircumcised. Paul's adversaries would probably respond that the division need not be there if all believers in Christ were to follow the law. Paul's vision, however, is of a single community of Gentiles and Jews in which Gentiles can remain as Gentiles. For Paul, law observance for Gentiles is a denial of the efficacy of Christ's death (2:21). For Paul, the only way for circumcised and uncircumcised believers to live is with the understanding that "in Christ Jesus neither circumcision nor uncircumcision has any value" (5:6). Paul's attitude to unity in Christ requires not that all Jews become Greeks or all Greeks become Jews but only that, whether Jew or Greek, all live in Christ.

Paul's record of his confrontation with Peter at Antioch speaks directly to the Galatian situation. Paul lets the Galatians know that in front of eminent Jewish Jerusalem Christians, he called even Peter to account. Paul now turns his attention to the Galatians' own experience of the power of the gospel.

## §12 Paul's Appeal to the Gospel the Galatians Have Known and Experienced (Gal. 3:1–5)

**3:1–2** / The apostle begins this section of his letter by addressing his readers as **foolish Galatians!** This designation appears to have been a common one for the Galatian tribes who were often considered barbarians and "foolish." The ancient Greek writer Callimachus (c. 305–c. 240 B.C.), for instance, uses the word as if it were a standard epithet, writing: "the foolish tribe of the Galatians" (*Hymn* 4, *To Delos* [Mair, LCL]).

Paul uses this epithet to remind the Galatians that they need not be as they once were and that in listening to the rival evangelists they are acting from their former ignorance instead of from their new life in Christ. In 3:3 he will repeat the word "foolish," where it is used to stress a turning away from what the Galatians know.

Paul is on the side of his converts, for he asks **Who has bewitched you?** To be bewitched is to be victim of someone's "evil eye," to be under another's spell. Paul is using language that will go straight to the pagan heart of his converts and thereby distance them somewhat from Jewish influence. Furthermore, Paul may have chosen the word "bewitch" to denigrate his opponents by casting them as magicians (see Betz, *Galatians,* p. 131). Here as elsewhere in the letter Paul does not deign to name his opponent(s).

The central and determining feature of the gospel for Paul is **Jesus Christ . . . crucified.** This is Paul's shorthand for reminding his readers of the gospel and that there is no need for Gentiles to adopt the law. As he said in the previous verse, "if righteousness could be gained through the law, Christ died for nothing!" For Paul, the death of Christ proves his point: the death of Christ means that the law is no longer the means by which to live for God or to live righteously.

Paul reminds the Galatians that while their vision may at the moment be obscured by their acceptance of a false gospel, they have seen the truth. For before their **very eyes** Jesus Christ

**was clearly portrayed as** crucified. Here Paul asserts what may be the very thing that his opponents are hiding—the scandal of the cross. Paul boldly identifies his gospel and the basis of his converts' faith with the crucifixion of Jesus Christ. Paul's gospel is a gospel that preaches the crucified one, who was unexpected, although continuous, with God's activity with the Jewish people. And Paul will go on to underscore for the Galatians that the truth of this gospel was demonstrated for them in their own experience—reception of the Spirit.

When Paul identifies his gospel with the cross he is identifying himself and believers in the gospel with a way of life that asks not for the certainty of rules or of social status but for the certainty of living in God, free to be for others because one is already crucified with Christ (2:20). Paul challenges his hearers to recognize that they have already acknowledged the power inherent in living a life that has died to the world. Their present desire to find security in the sign of circumcision and identification with the Jewish nation can only be explained as a form of bewitchment.

Paul further appeals to the Galatians on the grounds of what resulted from believing his gospel—he asks them how they received the Spirit. Paul presents his question respectfully: he wishes, he says, **to learn** from the Galatians. Having just called them "foolish," this is a remarkable rhetorical move. Paul indicates that he is on their side and is committed to them despite their actions at the moment. The **one thing** he wishes to learn is: **Did you receive the Spirit by observing the law, or by believing what you heard?** Obviously the Galatians received the Spirit through believing his gospel; there is no need, then, for adding the law. Paul constructs this question by setting up a mutually exclusive contrast between "observing the law" and "believing." In the Greek the contrast is even more evident. The syntactical constructions are exactly parallel in the first ("observing the law"; *ex ergōn nomou*) and second ("believing what you heard"; *ex akoēs pisteōs*) phrases.

This is the first time in the letter that Paul refers to the Spirit, who will become a central feature of his appeal to his Galatian converts. He will remind them not only that they received the Spirit at the beginning of their Christian life (3:3) but also that this is to be understood as a sign of a new stage in God's plan of salvation. As he says in 3:14, the promise to Abraham is fulfilled in the reception of the Spirit. To remind the Galatians that they have received the Spirit is to remind them that their experience marks them as those who are partaking in the fulfillment of God's promise.

Paul refers to the Spirit also when speaking positively about the character of the Christian life. The Spirit is in the hearts of believers (4:6); the Spirit accompanies, encourages, and undergirds our faith as we wait for the hope of righteousness (5:5). In fact, the Spirit is the life and guide of the Christian (5:25).

**3:3–5** / Paul asserts that the Galatian believers have continued confirmation that God is at work among them apart from their following the law. The one who gave them **his Spirit and work**[s] **miracles among** them does so because they **believe what** they **heard** (3:5), not because they observe the law.

Paul stresses **God** as the one who supplies the Spirit and works miracles. Both Paul and his converts around the Mediterranean world experienced the gospel as a gospel of power, accompanied, as Paul says in Romans, "by the power of signs and wonders . . . the power of the Spirit" (Rom. 15:19).

The Spirit is central to the Galatians' self-understanding of their Christian life. Both Paul and the Galatians can agree that they received the Spirit, and neither of them want to downplay such an experience. This may be one of the features of the Christian life upon which Paul and the Galatians can still agree, and so on the basis of the Galatians' experience of the Spirit Paul seeks to persuade them not to adopt the law.

The phrase "believe [believing] what you heard" occurs twice (3:2, 5), both times in opposition to "observe [observing] the law." The ability to hear means the Christian stands in the tradition of the OT figures who heard the word or the revelation of the Lord. Hearing means more than noting that something has been spoken; it means understanding and responding to what is heard (cf. Rom. 10:16; 1 Thess. 2:13). It bears the same meaning in Paul and in the rest of the NT (e.g., Mark 4:23; 1 John 1:1; Heb. 2:3) as in our modern context when a person might say "I hear you," meaning "I accept what you are saying." The phrase "believe what you heard" emphasizes that the activity of the Christian is to believe. This way of being open to God's revelation, to being shaped and transformed by conforming to Christ, is characteristic of the Christian life.

Paul repeats that the Galatians are exhibiting sheer folly **(are you so foolish?)** in being influenced by the rival evangelists.

To follow the direction of these people will mean that the spiritual journey begun with and characterized by the divine Spirit will be reduced to mere **human effort.**

Paul appeals to what the Galatians have already invested in their Christian life—**have you suffered so much for nothing?** The word "suffer" has two possible meanings: neutral experience, and suffering. Although there is no indication in the letter that the Galatians had experienced persecutions, it very likely that they paid a social cost as a result of their conversion. Beyond appealing to his converts' positive experience of the Spirit (3:5), Paul appeals to the fact that they have already experienced losses on account of the gospel. How foolish it would be now to lose the gospel also; then they would have suffered for nothing and would end up with nothing.

Nevertheless, Paul still holds out hope that the Galatians will come to their senses—**if it really was for nothing.** The emphasis in this construction is on "if." Paul is doubtful that the Galatians could turn away from his gospel. He hopes that they will recognize the significance of the fact that **God**'s miraculous activity among them did not result from following the law. Their new attraction to the law cannot garner them anything more wonderful than what they currently have—the Spirit and righteousness.

---

### Additional Notes §12

---

**3:1** / R. B. Hays has made clear how Paul's reference to "Jesus Christ crucified" is both the central point of the story of Jesus and the image capable of reminding his hearers of the whole gospel. As Hays puts it, the phrase "Jesus Christ crucified" "would be meaningless outside the frame of reference provided by the gospel story, [it] stands for the whole story and distills its meaning" (*The Faith of Jesus Christ*, p. 197).

Crucifixion in the Greco-Roman world was the form of capital punishment used almost exclusively for society's less privileged. It was rare for a Roman citizen or a wealthy person to be executed by means of this barbaric form of execution, except in the most extreme cases of high treason (see M. Hengel, "Crucifixion," in *The Cross of the Son of God* [trans. J. Bowden; London: SCM, 1986], pp. 93–185). As Hengel notes, the Roman government used crucifixion as a means of social control: "the chief reason for its use was its allegedly supreme efficacy as a deterrent" (ibid., p. 179). This form of public, lengthy, excruciating death was a warning against civil disobedience.

Hengel suggests that "the earliest Christian message of the crucified messiah demonstrated the 'solidarity' of the love of God with the
unspeakable suffering of those who were tortured and put to death by
human cruelty" (ibid., p. 180). N. Elliott argues that Paul's conversion to
the crucified Messiah was at the same time a "conversion to the cause of
the crucified" (*Liberating Paul: The Justice of God and the Politics of the
Apostle* [Maryknoll, N.Y.: Orbis, 1994], p. 227). That is, Paul became at
once committed to Christ and to society's poor and disenfranchised.
Elliott regards the centrality of the cross to Paul's gospel as a symbol of
his political commitment, or to put it another way, his commitment to
preaching God's justice. This is one of the reasons that Paul seeks to cre-
ate a community of equals that includes slave and free, male and female, Jew and Greek.

**3:2** / Paul sets up a contrast between **observing the law** and
**believing.** The phrase "observing the law" is a translation of the Greek
phrase *ergoi nomou* ("works of law"). This Pauline phrase has been vari-
ously understood. M. Luther interpreted the phrase to mean "good
works" and used the phrase to criticize the religious practice of his day.
R. Bultmann described "works of law" as "the righteousness which man
exerts himself to achieve" in distinction from "the righteousness from
God which is conferred upon him as gift by God's free grace alone"
(*Theology of the New Testament* [trans. K. Grobel; New York: Charles
Scribner's Sons, 1955], p. 285). In a somewhat similar vein D. P. Fuller
suggests that the phrase "represents an all-out rebellion against God"
because the law could be "in service of sin (and cause) a man to sin and
gratify his ego" (*Gospel or Law: Contrast or Continuum?* [Grand Rapids:
Eerdmans, 1980], p. 96). L. Gaston suggests that " 'works of law' is a normal subjective genitive" and so means that the law is the means by
which works are done ("Works of law as a subjective genitive," *Studies
in Religion* 13 [1984], pp. 39–46). J. D. G. Dunn argues that by "works of
law" Paul means all that the law requires of those who are bound by it.
The phrase refers not so much to works done seeking to earn God's
favor but to observances that mark the Jewish people off from other
people. "Works of law" are the "badges" that distinguish God's people,
so the phrase refers to "works which betoken racial prerogative" ("The
New Perspective on Paul," p. 200). E. P. Sanders states that "in the
phrase 'not by works of law' the emphasis is not on *works* abstractly conceived but on law, that is, the Mosaic law" (*Paul, the Law and the Jewish
People,* p. 46; italics his). S. Westerholm argues that the phrase "works of
law" refers to the same thing as the Mosaic law, for since the Mosaic law
required works this phrase referred simply to the law (*Israel's Law and
the Church's Faith: Paul and His Recent Interpreters* [Grand Rapids: Eerdmans, 1988], p. 121). The two latter interpretations make most sense of
the phrase since they see "works of law" as another way of saying
Torah.

## §13 Paul's Rebuttal of the Rival Evangelists' Use of the Example of Abraham (Gal. 3:6–9)

**3:6** / Next Paul turns from the Galatians' experience to Scripture. Citing the example of Abraham, Paul claims that just as Abraham had **credited to him . . . righteousness** on the basis of faith, so have the Galatians. This example is essential and strategic for Paul. It is essential because his opponents were probably using the story of Abraham in service of their position, for with Abraham God made the covenant of circumcision (Gen. 17:9–14). The story of Abraham would then provide the perfect warrant for the rival evangelists' contention that belief in Jesus Christ, the Jewish Messiah, entailed adopting the Jewish lifestyle and signifying that with circumcision. It was essential for Paul to counter this straightforward and seemingly irrefutable argument if he was to convince the Galatians of the truth of his law-free gospel.

Abraham is a strategic example for Paul because he can argue that Abraham was counted righteous before the covenant of circumcision. Quoting Genesis 15:6, Paul asserts that the fact that Abraham **believed God** led to God reckoning him as righteous. The rival evangelists would have been puzzled by Paul's separation of righteousness from obeying the dictates of the law. Paul, however, argues that righteousness through faith is defensible on the basis of Scripture and that righteousness by faith is at the root of the Jewish faith. Paul claims that his gospel, rather than that of his opponents, attests to the steadfastness of God and truthfully reflects God's intention.

To the Jews **Abraham** was the father of Israel to whom God gave the land (Ezek. 33:24). God was loyal to Abraham in a special way (Micah 7:20), even calling him "my friend" (Isa. 41:8), for God had made a covenant with Abraham and Abraham's descendants that God continually honored (Exod. 2:24; 4:5; 32:13). God chose Abraham to play a special role in the world because of Abraham's trust in God (Gen. 15:6).

Within Jewish tradition Abraham's righteousness is underscored. For instance, we read in *Jub.* 23:10: "For Abraham was perfect in all of his actions with the Lord and was pleasing through righteousness all of the days of his life" (trans. Wintermute; in *Old Testament Pseudepigrapha*). Jewish literature connects Abraham's righteousness with his faithfulness. In 1 Maccabees 2:51–52 Mattathias says to his sons: "Remember the deeds of the ancestors. . . . Was not Abraham found faithful when tested, and it was reckoned to him as righteousness?" And throughout Jewish tradition Abraham's faithfulness is connected with his keeping of the covenant. In the book of the scribe Jesus Ben Sira, Abraham is spoken of as "the great father of a multitude of nations. . . . He kept the law of the Most High, and entered into a covenant with him; he certified the covenant in his flesh, and when he was tested he proved faithful" (Sirach 44:19–20). As this final citation demonstrates, the covenant was signified by circumcision.

Thus Jewish tradition does not separate Abraham's faith from his keeping of the law. For the Jews the two are of a piece. Abraham is faithful and so he is righteous, being circumcised and keeping the law. Paul appears to be the first Jew to separate Abraham's faith from circumcision; his belief in God from law observance.

One of the most helpful contributions of recent Pauline scholars has been a new perspective on the Judaism out of which Paul came. The shorthand for this new perspective is "covenantal nomism." This term signifies that the Jews understood their relationship to God to be based on God's grace. God chose Israel and made a covenant with this nation. The law (nomism) was the way God laid out for Israel to know God's will and demonstrate gratitude and loyalty to God (see esp. E. P. Sanders, *Paul and Palestinian Judaism,* p. 75). The significance of this perspective is that it corrects the Christian view of Judaism as a religion that didn't understand God's grace and regarded the law as a way to salvation. Rather, the covenantal nomism of Judaism understood that God's gracious election of Israel assured Israel's salvation and that Israel's following of the law was an expression of gratitude and desire to stay within the covenant.

What distinguishes Paul from his Jewish kinfolk is not only that he argues against covenantal nomism but also that he separates grace (covenant) from law (nomism). Paul separates the response of faith to God's grace from the response of obeying the law; this in turn separates him from Judaism.

**3:7–9** / The rival evangelists were almost certainly using the story of Abraham to contend that unless the Galatians were circumcised they were not true heirs of Abraham. Paul turns this around and says that those who believe **are children of Abraham.** In Paul's view his case is clear from the evidence in Scripture, where it was foreseen **that God would justify the Gentiles by faith.** In other words, Paul asserts that he has Scripture on his side. Implicit in Paul's use of the passage from Genesis is a warning that those who do not agree with him are outside the circle of blessing. In Genesis 12 God makes this promise to Abraham: to "bless those who bless you; and the one who curses you I will curse." As Paul is convinced that only those who have faith through his law-free gospel are heirs of Abraham (3:7), it follows that those who are attacking that gospel are attacking also the true heirs of Abraham and so are cursed by God. Paul here infers what he said plainly in the opening of his letter—"if we or an angel from heaven should preach a gospel other than the one we preached to you, let him be eternally condemned!" (1:8; cf. 1:9).

Paul's exegesis would be seen by the rival evangelists as a misconstrual of the biblical text. In Genesis the promise to Abraham occurs three times, only once prior to the covenant of circumcision (Gen. 12:3). Within OT Scripture the promise is to be understood as a promise that takes for granted the covenant of circumcision, rather than, as Paul presents it, one that is independent of that covenant. The rival evangelists might further have taken issue with Paul on the basis that the word "Gentiles" is not found in Genesis 12 but only in the later passages (Gen. 18:18; 22:18). The precovenant promise in Genesis 12:3 has rather "peoples" (often correctly translated "tribes"), which does not serve Paul's purpose of making a direct connection between this text and the gospel he preaches to the Gentiles.

Moreover, Paul's opponents may legitimately have found it hard to understand how Paul could find scriptural support for his contention that the Scripture foresaw that God would justify the Gentiles by faith. In Genesis the Gentiles are promised blessing, not justification. And when in other parts of Scripture there is an expressed hope for the inclusion of the Gentiles it is inclusion into the covenant (e.g., Isa. 56:6).

Nevertheless, Paul considers himself to have Scripture on his side. Here as elsewhere, Paul interprets Scripture with the understanding that he has been granted authority to see clearly its meaning since, as he says in 1 Corinthians 10:11, "These things . . . were written down as warnings for us, on whom the fulfillment of the ages has come." In the face of his opponents Paul boldly asserts that those who believe are the descendants of Abraham.

Paul appeals to his converts' self-perception as **those who believe,** which later he will use effectively in distinction from those "who rely on observing the law" (3:10). The Greek phrase *hoi ek pisteōs,* which reads literally "those who are of faith" (the Greek of 3:10, *hosoi . . . ex ergōn nomou,* is literally "those of works of law") conveys the sense that there is a recognized group of people who distinguish themselves as believers. Earlier in the letter Paul can speak of "the faith" (1:23), expecting his readers' sympathetic attachment to that word. Paul now works his argument on the basis of his readers' self-understanding as "those who believe" (see also 3:9, where **those who have faith** is a translation of the Greek phrase *hoi ek pisteōs,* which is identical to the one in 3:7, translated "those who believe"). Since his addressees are "those who believe," they are children of Abraham.

The Greek reads literally "sons of Abraham," resonating with 3:26 ("sons of God"). The significance of "son" in this context is that it highlights the metaphor of inheritance, since in the ancient world the son was the inheritor of the father's legacy. The words **understand, then** should be read imperatively. Paul is commanding the Galatians to recognize what they have already implicitly accepted about themselves and to understand the consequences of such self-understanding: because they are believers they are sons of Abraham.

The curious phrase **the Scripture foresaw** is a way of saying that God foresaw (cf. Rom. 9:17). Paul, along with other Jews, could refer to Scripture speaking or acting. In the Mishnah (*Kerithoth* 6:9) it reads: "R. Simeon says: Everywhere Scripture speaks of sheep before goats. . . . Everywhere Scripture speaks of the father before the mother" (trans. Danby, p. 572). It was understood that when Scripture spoke or acted, God spoke or acted.

In Paul's interpretation of the Scriptures, Abraham is the first recipient of **the gospel** that Paul now preaches—a gospel in which "God would justify the Gentiles by faith." This is a powerful rhetorical move on Paul's part: he claims Abraham as not only the first one to enact the gospel of justification by faith (3:6) but also as the first one to know about it (3:8). The good news that God declares to Abraham is that **all nations will be blessed through you.** The Greek reads "in you" *(en soi).* Being "in Abraham" is to benefit from (be **blessed . . . with** [3:9]) Abraham's character and position. Being "in Abraham" is to be faithful (3:9) and righteous (3:6).

Paul wraps up and pulls together his thought by stating that believers are blessed along with Abraham. By referring to blessing Paul neatly deals with one of the problems his earlier use of the Scripture has caused—that in Genesis the Gentiles are promised blessing not justification. But he makes clear that he understands that the blessing is to be shared along with Abraham, who is **the man of faith,** the one who believed and so is righteous (3:6).

---

### Additional Notes §13

---

**3:6** / Paul here includes a quotation of Gen. 15:6. Most often Paul introduces or concludes scriptural citations with a phrase such as "for it is written" or "as Scripture says" (e.g., Gal. 3:13). In this verse Paul gives no indication that he is quoting Scripture. We see this also at Gal. 3:11.

Paul generally uses the Septuagint. When Paul diverges from the Septuagint scholars explain this as either due to his using a version of the biblical book to which we no longer have access or because he, like many other ancient authors, changed the quotation to suit his purposes. Within the Jewish tradition, reinterpretation and rewriting of Scripture was commonplace.

On Paul's use of Scripture, see A. T. Hanson, *The New Testament Interpretation of Scripture* (London: SPCK, 1980); E. E. Ellis, *Paul's Use of the Old Testament* (Edinburgh: Oliver & Boyd, 1957; repr., Grand Rapids: Baker, 1981); R. B. Hays, *Echoes of Scripture in the Letters of Paul* (New Haven: Yale University Press, 1989); and M. D. Hooker, "Beyond the Things That Are Written? St. Paul's Use of Scripture," in *From Adam to Christ: Essays on Paul* (Cambridge: Cambridge University Press, 1990), pp. 139–54. For Paul's argument about grace and law, see J. D. G. Dunn, "The Theology of Galatians: The Issue of Covenantal Nomism," in *Pauline Theology* (ed. J. M. Bassler; Minneapolis: Fortress, 1994), 1.125–46.

For an excellent overview of Abraham in Jewish writings, see G. W. Hansen, *Abraham in Galatians: Epistolary and Rhetorical Contexts* (Sheffield: Sheffield Academic Press, 1989), Appendix 2.

**3:8** / Paul's scriptural citation does not follow exactly Gen. 12:3, which reads "and all peoples on earth will be blessed through you." It appears that Paul has conflated Gen. 12:3 with Gen. 18:18 ("all nations on earth will be blessed through him") and perhaps also with Gen. 22:18 ("through your offspring all nations on earth will be blessed, because you have obeyed me"). Paul may have chosen to use Gen. 12:3 primarily while adding features from the other two passages because for his argument he needed a scriptural passage that occurred prior to the story about God requiring circumcision (Gen. 17), and he wanted to work with the contrast of blessing and curse that occurs in Gen. 12:3 ("I will bless those who bless you, and whoever curses you I will curse").

## §14 Why Gentile Christians Should Not Follow the Law (Gal. 3:10–18)

**3:10** / Paul now turns to a direct attack on following the law. He takes the tack that following the law is a denial of the truth of the gospel, and those **who rely on observing the law are under a curse.** Citing the curse from Deuteronomy 27:26, which ends a series of curses and precedes a list of blessings, Paul characterizes as under a curse those who are "of works of law" (the literal translation of the phrase "observing the law").

In one way Paul's use of Deuteronomy respects the passage's intention: the passage does promise a curse for those who do "not uphold the words of this law by carrying them out" (Deut. 27:26). Paul understands full well that the intention of the Jewish lifestyle is to fulfill the entire law. When he states in 5:3 that "every man who lets himself be circumcised . . . is obliged to obey the whole law," he demonstrates his grasp of the situation.

In another way, however, Paul's use of the passage is at odds with its function in Deuteronomy. Whereas the Deuteronomy passage functions to encourage obedience to the law, Paul uses it to warn against law observance. The result of becoming a full proselyte through circumcision means accepting the proposition that not observing the law (to which one is now committed) is to be under a curse.

This verse contains the first of four scriptural quotations arranged in a chiastic structure. The first and fourth (3:13) have parallel language, as do the second (3:11) and third (3:12).

> 3:10 *cursed is everyone* (who does not obey the law)
> 3:11 (the righteous) *will live* (by faith)
> 3:12 (the man who follows the law) *will live* (by the law)
> 3:13 *cursed is everyone* (who is hung from a tree)

The semantic effect of the chiastic arrangement of the scriptural quotations is to move from speaking of the law's curse on those who do not fulfill the obligations of the law (3:10) to the law's statement that the righteous one is the one who lives by faith (3:11) to the problem that the law requires those who participate in law to live by works of law (3:12) to the solution that Christ provided redemption from the curse by becoming a curse (3:13).

The fact that there is so much Scripture in this passage suggests that Paul is countering the use the troublemakers had made of these Scriptures. It is easy to see how at least three of the four scriptural quotations (Deut. 27:26; Lev. 18:5; Deut. 21:23) could have been put to good use by the rival evangelists.

**3:11** / When Paul states **clearly no one is justified before God by the law** his evidence is not phenomenological. That is, he does not cite the evidence of his or others' experience. Rather, Paul cites Scripture: **"The righteous will live by faith."** There are few other places where we see Paul the exegete so hard at work. Paul's argument does not rest on an assumption that humans find it impossible to fulfill the law. Rather, Paul's argument is based on the assumption that Scripture has something to say to the problem at hand, on the conviction that he rightly understands what it says, and on the desire to discredit whatever his opponents may have said on the basis of these Scriptures.

Paul is faced with the challenge of a seeming contradiction in Scripture. N. Dahl's suggestion makes good sense of Paul's use of Scripture in this passage. According to Dahl, Paul here uses legal arguments common among rabbis who sought to deal with contradictions in Scripture. When they were confronted with contradictory scriptural passages the rabbis sought to determine which passage held the basic principle that would serve to set the other passage in context. Paul sees an opposition between Habakkuk 2:4 ("the righteous will live by faith") and passages such as Deuteronomy 27:26 and Leviticus 18:5 ("the man who does these things [i.e., observing the law] will live by them"). Dahl proposes that the way Paul resolves the contradiction is to determine that the valid principle is "by faith" (Gal. 3:13–14). This means that the other scriptural principle, "by law," is provisional (Gal. 3:15–19; "Contradictions in Scripture," in *The Crucified Messiah and Other Essays* [Minneapolis: Augsburg, 1974], pp. 159–77).

**3:12** / Paul both reappraises his Jewish heritage in light of Christ and critiques it. He understands that fundamental to Judaism is faith. His use of Abraham demonstrates this more clearly than anything else could. For Jews, Abraham occupies the preeminent place he does with God and for God's people because he responded to God's call, because he trusted God; therefore, the Jewish people were founded on the basis of faith. Paul's reappraisal of Judaism consists in separating faith from law observance (see comments on 3:6). He writes: **the law is not based on faith.** Paul's critique of Judaism is that the life it may provide is only life under law— the one who practices law can do nothing but **live by** law. Paul's view is that since the coming of Christ such a way of life is seriously flawed. Now the law has been separated from faith, and it is with faith, not the law, that righteousness comes.

**3:13** / Paul believes that the change in the relationship between law and faith within Judaism results from Christ's death, which Paul interprets in various ways throughout his letters. As M. D. Hooker has noted, none of the images Paul uses to speak about the cross "is complete in itself" (*Not Ashamed of the Gospel: New Testament Interpretation of the Death of Christ* [Carlisle: Paternoster, 1994], p. 45). Here it serves the apostle's purpose to interpret Christ's death as one in which Christ became **a curse.** This description should be understood in the context of the following scriptural quotation. Paul uses metonymy: Christ did not become as the law is **(the curse of the law);** Christ took on the position of those under the law—he became accursed. Citing Deuteronomy 21:23, Paul describes Christ's death as one who was accursed, cut off from his people and from God. This place of curse is one that Paul and others were in until Christ **redeemed** them. Through his death Christ delivered believers from the "curse of the law" and thereby severed the relationship between faith in him and law. There is no need to follow law, for those who believe in Christ are released from law.

The quotation from Deuteronomy 21:23 contains the word "curse," as did the first quotation (3:10, citing Deut. 27:26). In the scriptural context of each quotation the word "curse" indicates exclusion from the community. In Deuteronomy 27:26 all the people say "amen" to the curse, thereby affirming their stand against the behavior cursed and their willingness to shun anyone disobeying the law. The context of the Deuteronomy 21:23 quote is instruction about the burial of a criminal's corpse: when someone is convicted of a crime punishable by death and so executed and hung on a tree, the corpse must not remain all night upon the tree but should be buried that day, for "anyone hung on a tree is under God's curse." The exposed corpse of a dead criminal would defile the land God gives as an inheritance. The language of curse in relation to Christ's death serves Paul's point of emphasizing that through the Galatians' faith in the death of Christ (3:1) they already are descendants of Abraham (3:7). He affirms that Christ's death released believers from the curse of potentially being excluded from the people of God and effected inclusion within the people of God for those in Christ.

Paul's use of Deuteronomy 21:23, in which the cursed person is a criminal deserving death, and his statement that Christ's death was in our stead (for us), make plain that Paul thinks that Christ died for our sins. Nevertheless, Paul does not say explicitly that Christ died for our sins; he does not state directly that Christ's death was a "sin offering" (cf. Rom. 8:3–4). The mechanics of salvation are beyond the rational realm. It is probably best to take Paul's words as metaphorical. He seeks to explain his conviction that Christ's death has effected the end of the law and opened the way for all to benefit from being the people of God. Paul's focus is not on the manner in which Christ's death made salvation available but on the fact that salvation is in Christ, apart from the law, and that those who believe in Christ are now incorporated into Christ.

Paul's use of the first person plural pronoun **us** does not indicate that the Galatians had been following the Jewish law before they came to faith in Christ. In fact, we know that they had been pagans (4:8). Rather, Paul is describing the stages of God's salvation plan, which he will describe in more depth in the subsequent verses. Before Christ everyone, Jew and pagan, was in slavery to the law (cf. 3:23), for whether one was a Jew or a pagan, there was no other way to deal with sin than through the law one knew (cf. Rom. 2:14). The ancient world understood law in a general sense to be that which reflected justice. As Aristotle says, " 'The just' therefore means that which is lawful or that which is equal and fair" (*Eth. nic.* 5.1.8 [Rackham, LCL]). Law was a way of measuring and achieving justice. By broadening the field to speak about law in general Paul asserts that the Galatians have already followed the law. This is an effective rhetorical strategy, for the conclusion is plain that through believing in Christ crucified (cf. 3:1), the Galatians have already once turned from following law.

**3:14** / Paul speaks of **the blessing given to Abraham** in the first instance, which accords with the scriptural passages.

Yet he immediately moves to his own interpretation of that blessing—**the promise of the Spirit.** It is this which Paul says **we ... receive ... by faith.** Whereas in 3:2 he had reminded his readers of what *they* had received, now Paul also affirms that he too has received the promise through faith. This shift is perhaps related to the fact that Paul directly relates reception of the promise to the death of Christ. As Paul tends to speak personally of the death of Christ as one in which he participates or one that is for him (2:20), it may be that Paul instinctively includes himself when speaking of Christ's death (3:13) and its consequences (3:14).

Paul says that **the promise** comes **through Christ Jesus.** The Greek reads not "through Christ," but "in Christ," *en Xristō.* This verse resonates with the scriptural quote in 3:8: "All nations will be blessed through [in] you." Just as God promised that *in* Abraham the nations would be blessed, so now it is *in Christ Jesus* that that blessing has come about. As R. B. Hays says about this verse: "It is only through *participation* in him that the Gentiles receive the blessing" (*The Faith of Jesus Christ,* p. 208).

The phrase **by faith** in the Greek is literally "through the faith" *(dia tēs pisteōs),* and it stands in parallelism with "in Christ Jesus." If a subjective genitive reading for 2:16 is adopted (see Introduction), the sense here would be "we receive the Spirit through the faith (of Christ) in which we participate by being in Christ, and we are in Christ because we are believers."

**3:15** / This is the first time since 1:11 that Paul addresses his readers as **brothers.** (This designation undoubtedly was meant to refer to both the male and female members of the Galatian churches.) He says that he wants to get at the issue at hand from the perspective of **everyday life.** Paul takes his example from the legal world and uses the case of a **human covenant.** His example turns out to be very brief, for he returns almost immediately to a discussion of Scripture.

On the basis of his distinctive understanding of the relationship of God's promise to Abraham and the giving of the law, Paul implicitly criticizes the rival evangelists for suggesting that in the law God has annulled God's promise that the righteous shall live by faith. This appears to be a response to what the troublemakers may have been preaching or what Paul understands as the consequence of their advocating of the law. Paul is convinced that the result of the rival gospel is to set aside or add to God's covenant with Abraham.

**3:16** / Paul takes up the matter of the **promises** that he introduced in 3:14. Normally Paul speaks of promise in the singular, as he did in 3:14, but in this verse and 3:21 he uses the plural (see also Rom. 9:4).

The biblical narrative has God making a promise to Abraham that concerns his offspring, or seed (Gen. 13:15; 17:7; 24:7), but Paul interprets these Scriptures to be saying that the promises were spoken both to Abraham and to the **seed**. His subsequent point emphasizing that "seed" is in the singular takes its significance from his interpretation that the promises were spoken to this seed, **who is Christ.** Such a reading of the Scripture bolsters his contention that through being "in Christ," the Galatians already have received the promise to Abraham (3:14). Since the promises were made both to Abraham and to Christ, those in Christ also inherit the promises to Abraham.

The word "seed," often translated "offspring," is found in Genesis 15:3, where Abram laments that God has given him no seed and so a slave shall be his heir. God promises that he will have a real heir and that Abram's legitimate descendants will be as numerous as the stars in heaven (Gen. 15:4–5). Because Abram believed this "the Lord . . . credited it to him as righteousness" (Gen. 15:6). Paul's reference to the promises made to Abraham and his offspring is an implicit reminder of Abraham's faith. Reference to the story of Abraham also foreshadows the story of Hagar and Sarah, a story to which Paul will turn later.

**3:17** / Paul starts to build his case for the priority of the covenant by noting that the law came much **later** than the covenant. Consequently, on the analogy of the example he used in verse 15, this has no effect on the original covenant.

Paul makes plain that his previous example from daily life (3:15) is to be applied to the issue of the relationship of the **covenant** and **the law** and of the Galatians' relationship to the **promise** to Abraham. The covenant is God's, and in referring to the covenant Paul is referring to the promise God gave to Abraham. Through repetition ("does not set aside"; "do away with") Paul stresses that it is false to think that God's law would **set aside** God's **covenant.** The covenant, the promise to Abraham, was not made void through God's giving of the law. In order to make his case against the rival evangelists Paul divides Abraham's faith from his obedience to the covenant. Now Paul makes a distinction between what in the Jewish mind was of a piece—the covenant and the law. The rival evangelists were likely arguing that the covenant included the law, that is, that obedience to the law was requisite for those who thought they were beneficiaries of the covenant. We see a similar understanding in Jewish Christian texts such as James 2:8–12 and the gospel of Matthew, where fulfilling the law through faith in Christ is an uncontested part of being a believer. Paul's stance is that the life of faith is at odds with obedience to the law, at least for Gentiles.

**3:18** / That Paul is shaping the argument on *his* terms is suggested further by the fact that here he works on the basis of a separation between **law** and **inheritance.** The following Sabbath prayer from the period of the Second Temple makes it plain that such a separation would have been foreign to the Jewish mindset, for the covenant, the law, and the inheritance were regarded as expressions of God's gracious love: "From thy love, O Lord our God, with which thou loved thy people Israel, and from thy compassion, our King, which thou bestowed on the sons of thy covenant, thou has given us, O Lord our God, this great and hallowed seventh day in love" (*t. Berakoth* 3.7; quoted from E. P. Sanders, *Paul and Palestinian Judaism,* p. 231). Yet Paul divorces the inheritance from the law. He argues that since the inheritance was given through the promise to Abraham and not through the law, then by implication if the Galatians are concerned about their inheritance they should focus on the promise instead of the law (cf. Rom. 4:16). By introducing the concept of inheritance Paul moves the argument forward. This concept will become increasingly important in his argument.

This is the only time in this letter that Paul uses the word *charizomai* (translated **gave**). In other letters this word occurs in the context of emphasizing God's gracious activity in Christ (Rom. 8:32) or in giving the Spirit (1 Cor. 2:12). Here Paul stresses that the inheritance promised to Abraham is based on nothing more or less than God's gracious gift. Implicit in this statement is that if the inheritance is shaped by gift and promise, then the Galatians are misguided to think that they can achieve it through a law-observant lifestyle.

## Additional Notes §14

**3:10** / The section of Scripture from which the first quotation is taken (Deut. 27:26) is sometimes referred to as the "Shechemite dodecalogue" since it records the twelve curses pronounced on Mount Ebal by Levites. Following the curses are blessings that were recited on Mount Gerizim (Deut. 28:1–6).

**3:13** / For a judicious overview of Paul's understandings of the death of Christ, see Hooker, *Not Ashamed of the Gospel*, pp. 20–46. See also J. T. Carroll and J. B. Green, " 'Nothing but Christ and Him Crucified': Paul's Theology of the Cross," in *The Death of Jesus in Early Christianity* (Peabody, Mass.: Hendrickson, 1995), pp. 113–32.

**3:15** / The example Paul chooses is difficult because within Greek and Roman law a **covenant** could be changed at any time. The Jewish law did have a covenant that could not be changed (so E. Bammel, "Gottes *DIATHEKE* (Gal. 3:15–17) und das jüdische Rechtsdenken," *NTS* 6 [July 1960], pp. 313–19). Yet, as Betz points out, it would be strange for Paul to be using such an example with his Gentile audience. Betz suggests that the practice of not changing a covenant may have been fairly widespread (*Galatians*, p. 155).

For a helpful analysis of Paul's response to the rival gospel, see C. H. Cosgrove, "Arguing Like a Mere Human Being: Galatians 3.15–19 in Rhetorical Perspective," *NTS* 34 (1988), pp. 536–49.

**3:16** / It was much more common in the Jewish than the Greek world to speak of God making **promises** to human beings. In the Greek world generally human beings made promises to God; see J. Schniewind and G. Friedrich, "*epangellō, epangelia*," *TDNT* 2:576–86, esp. pp. 578–79.

**3:17** / Exod. 12:40 states that the captivity of Israel in Egypt, that is, the time between Abraham and Moses, was **430 years.** The prediction to Abraham in Gen. 15:13 (cf. Acts 7:6) states that the captivity will be 400 years. Longenecker suggests that Paul may be following current rabbinic treatment of this discrepancy, which considered that while the captivity in Egypt was 400 years there were 430 years between God's covenant with Abraham and the Mosaic law (*Galatians*, p. 133).

## §15 The Limited Function of the Law in God's Purposes (Gal. 3:19–25)

**3:19** / Now Paul asks the question that he presumes his hearers must be asking: **What, then, was the purpose of the law?** Paul's answer is that he does consider the law to have had a purpose—**it was added because of transgressions.** But this purpose was time limited **until the Seed . . . had come.** Paul's answer underscores his previous argument that the fundamental and unchanging basis of God's relationship to God's people is the covenant with Abraham—**the promise.** The law's role, however, was not an eternal part of God's overall purpose; it had a beginning (430 years after the covenant; 3:17) and an end (the coming of the seed). This verse resonates with 3:16, in which Paul affirms that the seed is Christ to whom, along with Abraham, the promise was made.

Paul's presentation of the relationship between the law and transgressions is somewhat at odds with what he says in Romans, where he states that it is through the law that knowledge of sin comes (Rom. 3:20), and "where there is no law there is no transgression" (4:15). This discrepancy is largely the result of the rhetorical function of each of the passages. In Romans Paul is arguing for justification through faith on the basis of the general principle that no one, not even Abraham, is justified through law. In service of this argument Paul in Romans observes that the law functions to make one aware of sin. In Galatians Paul argues that the covenant with Abraham serves to structure all God's dealings with humanity. In order to make this argument Paul observes that the law was added after the covenant for the good purpose of dealing with transgressions, and he asserts that this purpose is completed with the coming of the "seed."

The Greek for **put into effect** (*diatageis*) is a participle of attendant circumstances, indicating that Paul is further describing his understanding of the circumstances surrounding the giving of the law. The participle is in the passive voice, and presumably God is the subject, just as at the beginning of the sentence God should be understood as subject of the passive verb "it was added" (cf. Williams, *Galatians*, p. 98). God directed the giving of the law to be **through angels.**

Most commentators take both Paul's reference to angels and to a **mediator** to be a deprecation of the law; God was absent at the giving of the law and it came through lesser beings. Yet, while Paul underscores the agency of the angels and the mediator in a way that is unique, the shape of his argument tells against understanding him to be indicating God's absence at the giving of the law. Paul's argument *against* the law works on the basis of a larger argument *for* the faithfulness of God. As his previous statements about the abiding nature of God's promise to Abraham demonstrate, Paul's basic position is that God's mind has not changed nor has God been absent during the course of salvation history. Paul's case is not built on proving a change or a flaw in God's historic relationship to God's people. Paul's case relies on the fact that God is faithful. Paul's argument would be undercut if he were saying that God was absent at the giving of the law: what good would a promise from such a God be?

The chief point Paul makes in 3:19 is that the law is time-limited and that it ended with the coming of the "seed" (Christ). His statement about the agency of angels and the mediator affirms the good purpose of the law, implicitly recalling his presupposition that God is trustworthy. Paul's use of the perfect tense (the tense often used in Greek to indicate a past action with continuing results in the present) for the verb, which is translated by the phrase "the promise . . . had come," provides corroborative evidence that Paul intends to stress the faithfulness of God to the promise. As he says later, the law is not at odds with God's promises (3:21).

Paul's statement about angels accords with the positive reference to the participation of angels at the giving of the law found in the NT (Acts 7:38, 53; Heb. 2:2) and in other Jewish writings. In these texts the presence of angels does not indicate the absence of God. Philo writes that angels "are represented by the lawgiver as ascending and descending: not that God, who is already present in all directions, needs informants, but that it was a boon to us in our sad case to avail ourselves of the services of 'words' acting on our behalf as mediators" (*On Dreams* 1.141–142 [Colson and Whitaker, LCL]). In the *Testaments of the Twelve Pa-*

*triarchs* an angel is spoken of positively as being the mediator between God and humanity for the peace of Israel (*Testament of Dan* 6:2). Josephus has Herod say "we have learned the noblest of our doctrines and the holiest of our laws from the messengers [angels] sent by God" (*Ant.* 15:136 [Marcus, LCL]).

**3:20** / Paul's statement that a **mediator** by definition cannot represent only one party works on the assumption that the mediator is a go-between and not the principal initiator of the transaction. As in the previous verse, so here Paul indicates his conviction that the law has a divine origin. Incorporating what may have been the rival evangelists' presentation of the glorious, angel-attended event of Moses' reception of the law, Paul declares that the mediator **does not represent just one party.** Paul contrasts the mediator with God. God, whom the Jewish faith affirms as **one** (Deut. 6:4), is the source of the law. The mediator was the agent through whom the law was given; the source of the law is God.

Typically commentators take this verse as Paul's further deprecation of the law, in which he stresses that the law came only indirectly from God. Yet if Paul were asserting this he would be hurting the fundamental premise he needs in order to argue that the revelation in Christ is continuous with salvation history—the faithfulness of God. Such an assertion would also contradict his immediately preceding statement that the law was divinely ordained (3:19). Paul does not want to denigrate the law; he wants to present it in accord with the fundamentals of the Jewish faith.

**3:21–23** / Paul brings to the forefront the question that has been underlying the whole discussion—**Is the law, therefore, opposed to the promises of God?** The fact that Paul asks the question as he does and answers it with **Absolutely not!** demonstrates again that Paul thinks the law finds its source in God. This is a different approach to the law from what we find in other early Christian writings, which, in light of the adequacy of Christ, declare the inadequacy of the law (e.g., Heb. 7:18–19; Justin Martyr, *Dial.* 11 [*ANF* 1.199–200]). It is also a different approach from that of Marcion, whom Ireneaus reports as divorcing the God proclaimed by the law and the prophets from the God revealed in Jesus Christ (*Against Heresies* 1.27.2; [*ANF* 1.352]). Rather, Paul understands the law as adequate for the role it was intended to play but regards that role as limited in both duration and function.

Paul has already said that the law's function had to do with transgressions (3:19), and now he says that its function is not to **impart life** or **righteousness.** The law and the promises do not contradict each other; they serve different purposes. The law's function cannot go beyond that of containing transgressions. God's gift of life and righteousness is what **was promised,** and it is available **through faith in Jesus Christ** or through the faith of Jesus Christ (see Introduction). The promise and the law are not in conflict. Rather, God intended their coexistence, at least for a time, within God's salvific dealings with humanity.

At this point Paul introduces into the discourse the idea of imparting life. At several points in his letters, when speaking of God's salvific activity in Christ, Paul uses the concept of "life" (e.g., Rom. 4:17; 8:11; 1 Cor. 15:22). For Paul, God is the giver of life, which entails much more than fleshly existence (1 Cor. 15:36, 45).

Paul uses **Scripture** as a metonymy for God, comparable to how he uses Scripture at 3:8. The Greek for **declares** *(synekleisen)* has the meaning of "confine" or "shut up," thereby suggesting that Scripture or God imprisons. The word occurs also at Romans 11:32, where God is the one who imprisons or confines all people in disobedience. Both references give evidence to one side of the theological tension, found in Paul and throughout the Bible, that arises from believing both in God's sovereignty and in human responsibility. In Galatians, in the context of stating that the law "was added because of transgressions" (3:19), Paul also asserts that even the cause of the law—sin—was under God's control. Paul declares something similar at the beginning of Romans, where he says that God hands sinners over to their sin (Rom. 1:28).

It has been suggested that "Scripture" should be understood as referring to a particular Scripture, as Paul does elsewhere (e.g., 3:8; 4:30), and that the Scripture to which Paul is referring is Deuteronomy 27:26 (so E. Burton, *A Critical and Exegetical Commentary on the Epistle to the Galatians* [International Critical Commentary; New York: Scribner, 1920], p. 195; and Longenecker, *Galatians,* p. 144). This makes "the Scripture" synonymous with "the law" of verse 19, for the reference to Deuteronomy 27:26 (v. 10) undergirds the claim in verse 19. Yet surely it would damage Paul's argument about the limitations of the law if in verse 22 he were claiming that the law/Scripture had the capacity to imprison sin. His point rather is that the law was used by God for a particular period of time for certain limited pur-

poses, a point he will reiterate in the following verse. Paul is referring to Scripture as that which testifies to the ways of God.
God, not the law or Scripture, is the implicit subject of verse 22.
When we look at the whole sentence, it is God who made the
promise **to those who believe.**

The second clause of the verse is a purpose clause describing the reason for which God imprisoned all things under sin. It
was **so that what was promised** might be given to those who believe "through faith in Jesus Christ." The promise, which is the
promise to Abraham, is a gift. In 3:14, Paul has qualified this as a
promise of the Spirit, which believers have already received.

If we take a subjective genitive reading for "through faith
in Jesus Christ" (see Introduction) the sense is that the promise is
given to those who believe with the faith of Jesus Christ. This is
another way of saying what Paul said in 3:14—that through or in
Christ Jesus the blessing of Abraham might come to the Gentiles,
so that they might receive the promise of the Spirit through faith.

At first it seems curious that Paul should now speak of faith
coming, since he has been seeking to prove that faith was always
a factor in God's dealings with God's people. If, however, he is
using faith as a shorthand way of referring to his statement in
verse 22 about the faith of Jesus Christ, then Paul is saying that
until the coming of Christ the law guarded human beings. Faith
is something that can be **revealed,** which attests to its hidden
presence in the period before its coming. This is different from
the act of believing in God, which Paul claims has always been
evident in the structure of the divine-human relationship (3:6–7).
The "faith" that is revealed, therefore, is not defined by the manner in which humans relate to God but by the person through
whom humans relate to God. As Wallis writes, "It seems probable . . . that Paul identifies the revelation of faith in 3:23 with the
coming of Christ" (*The Faith of Jesus Christ in Early Christian Traditions,* p. 113). The faith in verse 23 is a synonym for the faith of
Christ that is clarified in the following verses, where Paul sets the
coming of faith in parallelism with being in Christ Jesus (vv.
25–26). The faith that is revealed is the faith of Jesus Christ in
whom, through faith, believers participate.

Continuing to answer the challenge "why then the law?"
Paul expands on what he has said in verse 22. Being "prisoner(s)
of sin," human beings **were held prisoners by the law.** Paul
repeats the thought of verse 19, that God brought in the law
because of transgressions. The divinely assigned role for the

law was that of confining sin for a period of time until faith should come.

**3:24** / Through his use of the word **so** Paul indicates that now he is giving a straightforward answer to the question he raised in verse 19. The law's purpose was custodial for the period before Christ. The law's function was both negative and positive, for while it confined (v. 23), it did so with a view to liberation. The law's role was to be **in charge** so **that we might be justified by faith.**

The Greek word translated by "in charge" (*paidagōgos*) means pedagogue, tutor, or guardian. In the ancient Greco-Roman world a pedagogue was a standard member of a well-to-do household. Pedagogues were the guardians in charge of educating and directing the ethical conduct of the sons of the household. Paul equates the law's function with that of guardianship. The metaphor suggests that as a guardian keeps watch over a child until the child reaches maturity, so the law guarded humanity until the coming of Christ. In the following verses Paul will appeal to the idea of inheritance (3:29–4:7), which is the flipside of the idea of guardianship. In the ancient world a boy often had a guardian until the age of maturity, at which point he came into his inheritance. In verse 24 Paul suggests that the way to understand the purpose of the law is as a time-limited guardian or disciplinarian, and he strongly implies that the opportunity of being "justified by faith" is akin to attaining maturity.

Throughout this passage faith refers to the action of believing (3:22b) and to the faith of Christ (3:23, 25), the one who has come. The second part of verse 24 fills out what Paul has said by claiming that the law served a purpose until Christ came. As a result of Christ's coming righteousness is available to all through faith. A believing response to the faith of Christ means that one is "in Christ," as Paul goes on to say in verse 26. Belonging to Christ in this way makes one an heir to the promise (v. 29). The age of maturity, in which the inheritance can be received, is available to those who live by faith in Christ. Being justified by faith is a sign that one is grown up, for it is a sign that one has inherited the promise to Abraham (3:6–9).

**3:25** / Paul brings this part of his argument to a climax by repeating that **faith has come** (cf. 3:23). Since this is so, the law's function of **supervision** is ended. Such a claim on Paul's part was a powerful retort to the rival evangelists' position that law observance was the appropriate completion to faith in Christ.

Rather than law observance being the sign of fully becoming part of the people of God, Paul argues, it is a sign that one is still a minor and so incapable of inheriting the promise to Abraham. Using the present tense Paul asserts that he and the Galatians are at the age of majority: **we are no longer under the supervision of the law.**

---

### Additional Notes §15

---

**3:19** / Paul, like other Jews, referred to Moses as **mediator;** see T. Callan, "Pauline Midrash: The Exegetical Background of Gal. 3:19b," *JBL* 99 (1980), pp. 549–67, esp. p. 555.

The Greek word for **angels** *(angelos)* can mean angels or messengers. In the Bible angels often have the role of fulfilling a commission on God's behalf, of communicating with significant people at turning points in Israel's history, e.g., with Hagar, Gen. 16:7; 21:17; with Moses when God's name is revealed, Exod. 3:2; and with the shepherds in the NT birth narratives.

Although there is an ambiguous reference in Deut. 33:2 to God's giving of the law being accompanied by angels (for translation of Deut. 33:2, see Martyn, *Galatians,* p. 357), the OT narratives about the giving of the law portray God speaking directly to Moses and generally do not mention angels (e.g., Exod. 19). As mentioned in this commentary, many take Paul's reference to angels and to a **mediator** to be a deprecation of the law (so Betz, *Galatians,* p. 171; Matera, *Galatians,* pp. 133–34; Longenecker, *Galatians,* pp. 141–43; J. D. G. Dunn, *A Commentary on the Epistle to the Galatians* [London: A & C Black, 1993], p. 191). See also W. D. Davies, who suggests that in order to counter the Christian claim that the law was an inferior revelation because of its mediation by angels, some rabbis made efforts "to belittle the role of the angels on Mt. Sinai" ("A Note on Josephus, Antiquities 15:136," *HTR* 47 [1954], pp. 135–40, esp. p. 140, n. 11).

The phrase **until the Seed . . . had come** may be a paraphrase of Gen. 49:10, which was often interpreted messianically (so D. Juel, *Messianic Exegesis: Christological Interpretation of the Old Testament in Early Christianity* [Philadelphia: Fortress, 1988], p. 86).

**3:20** / By boldly asserting the fundamental Jewish conviction that **God is one** (Deut. 6:4), thereby putting himself in line with the basic faith of Judaism, Paul continues to underscore his point that his gospel is continuous with Judaism. This is the same function that reference to the Shema (God is one) plays in Rom. 3:28–31—to stress that Paul's gospel is the outworking of Judaism, even of God's giving of the law.

For an interpretation that in some regards is complementary to the one given here, see N. T. Wright, who understands Paul to be affirming the divine origin of the law while at the same time considering that "the law cannot be God's final word." For Wright the key to Paul's argument is his conviction that the unity of God means that God desires also a single family. The problem with the law is that it was given to one race only. The law, therefore, had temporary status in God's plan. ("The Seed and the Mediator: Galatians 3.15–20," in *The Climax of the Covenant: Christ and the Law in Pauline Theology* [Minneapolis: Fortress, 1993], pp. 157–74).

**3:21** / As noted, the standard interpretation of Paul's point in vv. 19–20 is that he wishes to show that the law is "intrusive, temporary, secondary and preparatory" (Bruce, *Galatians*, 179). In such an interpretation v. 21 is seen as a question to which the reader might rightly expect an affirmative answer (ibid., p. 180). However, the fact that Paul raises the question in order to answer it with an emphatic denial suggests again that Paul's point in the previous verses, rather than being to point out the inferior origin of the law, is to claim only that the law has a circumscribed function in God's dealings with humanity. The law is limited in terms of time and of function.

The Greek for **Absolutely not!** *(mē genoito)* is the standard emphatic rebuttal used in persuasive arguments of the time. See Epictetus: "Now that three things belong to man, soul, and body and things external . . . all you have to do is answer the question which is best? . . . The flesh? . . . 'God forbid'! ["absolutely not"]" (*Arrian's Discourses* 3.7. 2–4 [Oldfather, LCL]).

**3:23** / Others also understand "the faith" to refer to Christ. See, for example, K. Stendahl, *Paul among Jews and Gentiles* (Philadelphia: Fortress, 1976), p. 21; R. Hays, *The Faith of Jesus Christ*, pp. 230–32; Martyn, *Galatians*, p. 122.

## §16 Gentiles Are Inheritors of God's Promise to Abraham through Being in Christ (Gal. 3:26–4:7)

**3:26** / The basis upon which Paul makes the previous statement in verse 25 is his conviction that the Galatians are **all sons of God** by virtue of their being **in Christ Jesus.** Paul continues to work with the metaphor of inheritance to underscore that all of his readers are inheritors of God's promise. Paul emphasizes that the Galatians already are "sons" or inheritors of God's promise. (Paul's use of "sons" is meant not to exclude the female members of the Galatian churches, but to work with the inheritance metaphor. In the ancient world it was generally sons and not daughters who could expect to be inheritors.) For the benefit of both his Gentile Galatian converts and the Jewish Christian troublemakers who would have eventually heard his words, Paul says that "all" receive the inheritance through the faith of Jesus Christ.

The Greek contains two consecutive prepositional phrases, *dia tēs pisteōs* and *en Christō Iēsou,* reading literally "through the faith" and "in Christ Jesus." By means of "the faith"—both the action of believing and the faith of Christ—all are "sons of God." And by being "in Christ Jesus" all are "sons of God." For Paul and the early Christians who proclaimed this confession "the faith" was synonymous with being "in Christ."

This verse introduces what many regard as a pre-Pauline baptismal formula (3:26–28). If this is the case, we have here one of the earliest Christian self-descriptions.

**3:27** / Paul declares that the Galatians have **clothed** themselves **with Christ.** A similar phrase occurs in Romans 13:14, in which being clothed in Christ is equivalent to avoiding "deeds of darkness." The metaphor of being clothed is used in other literature of Paul's time for putting on virtue (e.g., Wisdom of Solomon 5:18). It is used in the Septuagint in connection with

receiving the Spirit (e.g., Judg. 6:34). The image of being clothed
with Christ becomes a feature of Christian hymns in the first century: for instance, in the *Odes of Solomon*, "In form he was considered like me, that I might put him on" (7:4; trans. Charlesworth).
Thus, being clothed with Christ is putting on Christ's character,
which is that of righteousness. Paul reinforces his claim that the
Galatians have no need to search for righteousness in any place
other than their present life in Christ. In a situation in which believers are being asked to take on the law, Paul calls these believers to recognize their new identity as those who are clothed with
Christ.

Paul appeals to his readers' having been **baptized.** Different religious groups or individuals in the ancient world used
water ablutions ritually, both Jews (e.g., John the Baptist, the
Qumran community, Bannus [see Josephus, *The Life* 11]) and
Gentiles (e.g., in the cults and mysteries of Eleusis, Isis, Bacchus,
and Mithras). The significance attached to this sacred washing
was different in each context. Even within early Christianity various understandings of baptism are in evidence. In some cases a
direct connection is made between baptism and the Holy Spirit
(Mark 1:8), in others between baptism and repentance (Acts
2:38). Paul speaks infrequently about baptism. It appears that he
considered his task primarily to be that of preaching (1 Cor. 1:17).
What he says in letters other than Galatians about baptism accords with what he says here—baptism is into Christ (Rom. 6:3)
and results in unity, even the unity between Jew and Greek,
slave and free (cf. 1 Cor. 12:13). Romans 6 elaborates on the claim
that baptism is baptism into Christ. Baptism is into Christ's death
(Rom. 6:3), which is a death for sin (Rom. 5:6–8) and which deals
with sin (Rom. 5:10). Being baptized into Christ saves one from
sin's power and allows one to become as Christ is—righteous.
Furthermore, baptism is a sharing in the drama of Christ. Through
baptism a person dies with Christ and hopes for resurrection
(Rom. 6:4). Paul's main point in Galatians 3:27 is, however, not to
describe what happens in baptism but to affirm that his readers
are "in Christ." Because they are in Christ they do not need to
add anything to their faith and may live in the freedom that belongs to heirs.

**3:28** / Being clothed with Christ results in a new self-
perception. The implication of this statement is that to regard
oneself or others primarily in ethnic (**Jew** or **Greek**), social (**slave**

or **free)**, or gender (**male** and **female**) terms is to use categories inappropriate to the present, for after the coming of faith, those who believe are "sons of God," "clothed with Christ," and "in Christ." For those Galatians "in Christ," the law, which maintains ethnic boundary lines and delineates social and gender distinctions, has no relevance. Paul makes statements similar to Galatians 3:28 in 1 Corinthians 12:13 and Colossians 3:11. These two other letters were written from and to circumstances different from those in Galatia, which suggests that this statement was an early and widely used description of the faith.

Only Galatians 3:28 contains the phrase neither **male nor female**. In the Greek the phrase stands out because it reads literally "male *and* female" in distinction from "Jew *nor* Greek," "slave *nor* free." The phrase exactly echoes the Septuagint of Genesis 1:27: God created man "male and female." Perhaps early Christians chose this phrase deliberately so as to signify that in baptism a new creation occurs (cf. 2 Cor. 5:17), one that redefines even the most basic features of the original creation.

The inclusion of the phrase "male nor female" in Galatians may be because of the issue of circumcision. In this regard it is interesting to read Justin Martyr, whose comments indicate the positive way that the church's rejection of circumcision could redound to women. Justin comments that

> the inability of the female sex to receive fleshly circumcision, proves that this circumcision has been given for a sign and not for a work of righteousness. For God has given likewise to women the ability to observe all things which are righteous and virtuous; but we see that the bodily form of the male has been made different from the bodily form of the female; yet we know that neither of them is righteous or unrighteous merely for this cause, but [is considered righteous] by reason of piety and righteousness. (*Dialogue with Trypho* 23 [*ANF* 1.206])

The center of gravity in the confession of 3:26–28 is Christ. Christ is the transformative locus of the faith the Galatians know. Through reference to what may have been a widely used baptismal confession, Paul reminds the Galatians of their initial understanding of the faith. Their original commitment was to a worldview in which they understood themselves to have gained a new identity, one rooted in and defined by Christ. This identity transcended all typical social distinctions and the moral distinctions that resulted from such social differentiating, and upon this shared understanding the affirmation in verse 29b is based. Paul expects the Galatians to fully embrace the self-understanding articulated in 3:27–29a, and so he uses it as another way to support his point that Gentiles are inheritors of the promise to Abraham without following the law.

**3:29** / Paul asserts that the Galatian believers **belong to Christ,** which means that they are **Abraham's seed.** The word "seed" is plural and brings to mind Paul's comments in 3:16. In that verse Paul argued that the promise was given to the singular "seed," Christ. Now Paul includes the Galatian believers in that promise on the basis of their belonging to Christ. The key element for receiving the promise of inheritance is whether or not one is "in Christ," or, as Paul puts it here, "belongs to Christ." Those who are in Christ are the **heirs.** Paul's use of the simple present tense, **you are,** highlights his desire to convince the Galatians to acknowledge and embrace the wondrous new life they have.

**4:1** / Paul now draws a tighter circle around the opponents of his gospel. Using the first person singular, which was more characteristic of the earlier part of the letter, he works with the concept of the heir. Paul points out that being an **heir** is not enough in and of itself, if the heir is still a **child.** While an heir theoretically owns **the whole estate . . . as long as the heir is a child, he is no different from a slave.** An inheritance is of no benefit unless one is an adult.

**4:2** / The minor lives neither freely nor fully. Rather, **he is subject to guardians and trustees until the time set by his father.** Paul equates the type of life advocated by the rival evangelists with the confining life of minors. His pregnant phrase "until the date set by his father" signals what he will declare in verse 4, that the appointed time is here.

**4:3** / In saying that the Galatians and he once **were children** Paul implies that in the present they are heirs. As minors are restricted by guardians and trustees, so humans without Christ **were in slavery under the basic principles of the world.** For Paul's point to have an impact he must expect the Galatians to have some appreciation of the negative aspect of the "basic principles of the world" *(stoicheia tou kosmou).* This suggests that the Galatians originally understood their new life as one of freedom from these "basic principles of the world." Paul's legal metaphor has moved into the existential realm.

Paul's statement that "we were in slavery," when it is read in conjunction with his qualification of the basic principles (*stoicheia*) as being of the world, suggests that he is making a statement about a general, widely held attitude. He is appealing to a worldview in which the human condition was seen as subject to the forces of the cosmos; this worldview was often accompanied by fear or fatalism. By implicitly equating being under the law with being enslaved to the "basic principles of the world," Paul finds another way to focus his readers' attention on the folly and danger of adding the law to faith in Christ.

**4:4** / Continuing with the concept of the time-limited purpose of the law, Paul writes that at a particular point, **when the time had fully come,** God ended the age of minority and the period of enslavement. With the coming of Jesus, when **God sent his Son,** a new period in God's salvation plan has begun (cf. Rom. 8:3). The implicit warning to the Galatian readers is that by adding the law to their faith they are going backwards and are becoming out of sync with God's plan.

Paul's use of the christological title "Son" resonates with the surrounding verses, in which he states that believers are also "sons of God." Paul underscores, perhaps by alluding to an already known christological formulation, that the Son of God is to be identified as the one **born of a woman, born under law.** His reference to Jesus' Jewish birth may be a retort to an argument of the rival evangelists. Jesus' Jewishness could well have been used to persuade Gentile converts to adopt Jewish practices. Paul here affirms the Son of God's Jewishness but with a view to a different outcome.

**4:5** / God sent God's Son so that **those under law** might be redeemed. The law's confining function is emphasized, as it was in 3:23. The role of Christ was **to redeem,** to buy out of slavery, those imprisoned under law (cf. 3:13). According to Paul, that which the Galatians are considering as an addition to their faith in Christ is the very thing that Christ was commissioned to bring freedom from. Christ's Jewishness is not a reason for believers to adopt the Jewish law. It is the means by which God brought in the new age of freedom from the law.

God also sent God's Son so as to allow the Galatians and other believers to receive **the full rights of sons.** Picking up the theme of inheritance and using a word for adoption (*huiothesian;* here translated "full rights") that in the Greek is built on the root "son," Paul states that through Christ God has made it possible for all believers to partake of the heritage of God's Son. Paul uses the concept of adoption to solve from another angle the problem of how Gentiles can be legitimate descendants of Abraham. His reference to Christ's Jewish birth in the previous verse is employed here to declare that now believers share in Christ's lineage, but not by being under law.

**4:6** / Using the present tense, Paul declares that his readers **are sons,** that is, they are the legitimate heirs.

Just as God sent the Son to do the work of redeeming those under the law, to allow for adoption (4:4–5), so **God sent the Spirit of his Son** into the hearts of all sons of God. The adoption is not only legal, for believers receive the Spirit of Christ so that they can authentically call God *"Abba,* **Father."** Paul affirms that God's work of adoption is a wholistic work: God makes it possible for believers to become God's legitimate children and to know themselves as such, through the Spirit.

In all likelihood Paul is referring to the Galatians' experience of the Spirit, to which he referred earlier (3:2–5). He uses this experience to demonstrate again that they already have all they could ever ask for. While the metaphor of legal minority has broken down by this point in Paul's argument, the present image of sons being able directly to address their father still works with the metaphor. Believers have gained special status with God and are no longer "subject" (4:2) to anyone else's authority. Through the spirit they know themselves to be what they are—children of God (cf. Rom. 8:15–16).

**4:7** / Paul brings his use of the inheritance metaphor to a conclusion by stating that now the Galatians should think of themselves as **a son.** The previous argument has demonstrated that to take on the law would be to become **a slave.** The key to receiving the inheritance is not to follow the Jewish law but to embrace what God has given them in Christ. Already, as children of God (4:6), **God has made** them **also an heir.** Paul's choice here of singular rather than plural nouns may be so as to indicate that the Galatians are now a people in a manner comparable to the OT's use of the singular "son" or "child" of God for Israel (e.g., Hos. 11:1). We see something similar elsewhere in the NT when believers are described as a people (1 Pet. 2:9).

## Additional Notes §16

**3:26** / The phrase translated as **through faith** is awkward in the Greek *(dia tēs pisteōs)*, reading "through the faith." The article is missing from a few important manuscripts (e.g., P46), which may indicate that early on scribes tried to smooth this grammatical clumsiness. Some have explained the awkwardness by suggesting that at this point Paul has inserted his own phrase into a preexisting confession.

**Sons of God** resonates with the idea of inheritance and with the Jewish conviction that Israel is the son of God (e.g., Exod. 4:22–23; Deut. 14:1–2; Hos. 11:1). Again Paul emphasizes that the Galatians, without observing the Torah, already have what the rival evangelists are promising.

**3:27** / For an overview and analysis of Paul's view of baptism as it relates to the reception of the Spirit, see J. D. G. Dunn, *Baptism in the Holy Spirit* (SBT, 2d series 15; London: SCM, 1970), pp. 103–72.

**3:28** / We know from both Greek and Jewish writing of the period that the categories to which Paul refers were seen to be the most fundamental. Diogenes Laertius attributes to Thales a thanksgiving "that I was born a human being and not one of the brutes; next, that I was born a man and not a woman; thirdly, a Greek and not a barbarian" *(Lives of Eminent Philosophers* 1.33). R. Judah b. El'ai (ca. A.D. 150) says: "There are three blessings one must pray daily: Blessed [art thou], who did not make me a gentile; Blessed [art thou], who did not make me a woman; Blessed [art thou], who did not make me an uncultured person" *(t. Berakoth* 7.18; cf. the Jerusalem Talmud, *Berakoth* 9.1). Paul's affirmation that all of these distinctions now become subsumed in Christ is a powerful way to express his vision of the faith.

**4:2** / Paul's legal analogy cannot be directly applied, for in most cases it was not a decision of the father but the law's provision that at a certain age—the end of the fourteenth year—a minor would inherit.

**4:3** / The phrase **basic principles of the world** is difficult to translate, since the word for "basic principles" *(stoicheia)* has several meanings on its own. The phrase "basic principles of the world" *(stoicheia tou kosmou)*, is rare in ancient Greek literature, although see Philo, who writes "we men are an amalgamation out of four elements ['basic principles'], which in their totality are elements of the universe [the Greek word could mean 'world']" *(On the Eternity of the World* 29 [Colson, LCL]). The Greek for "basic principles," *stoicheia*, means "what belongs to a series" (G. Delling, "*stoicheion*," *TDNT* 7:670–87, esp. p. 670) and was used, for instance, when referring to the series of sounds in the alphabet. To participate in a series is to follow a certain order or to be guided. The same word is found in verbal form in Gal. 6:16 for following ("follow this rule") and at 5:25; "let us keep in step with the Spirit." For a comprehensive discussion, see Burton, *Galatians,* pp. 510–18.

When used as a noun in 4:3 and 4:9 *stoicheia* has the sense of elements, rudiments, or basic principles, the "smallest parts which stand in relation with others" (Delling, *TDNT* 7:678). The word came to be used particularly in Stoicism to refer to the belief that the cosmos was made of four basic elements. All of matter could be explained as based on the four elements of earth, water, air, and fire. The ancients had various attitudes to these elements. Isis was thought to be a diety who controlled the "basic principles" (Apuleius, *Metamorphoses* 11.1). Devotion to Isis provided protection from the *stoicheia.* See 2 Pet. 3:10 for how the end of days is connected with the destructive force of the elements. According to Clement of Alexandria, the philosophers wrongly ascribed divine qualities to the *stoicheia* (*Exhortation to the Greeks* 5.1).

Others considered them to be the elements out of which all is created and so the source of basic humility; every creature will be destroyed by the elements and return to them. Philo has the elements speaking to human beings, saying "we it is whom nature blended and with divine craftsmanship made into the shape of human form. Out of us you were framed when you came into being and into us you will be resolved again when you have to die" (*On the Special Laws* 266 [Colson, LCL]). The word also came to be connected with "star" or "constellation" and consequently was at times related to an understanding that the stars or elements influence the course of events. On this see B. Reicke, "The Law and This World According to Paul: Some Thoughts Concerning Gal. 4:1–11," *JBL* 70 (1951), pp. 259–76. Delling suggests that for Paul the elements represent "that whereon man's existence rested before Christ . . . that which is weak and impotent, that which enslave man instead of freeing him" (*TDNT* 7:685).

**4:4** / This is the only place in Paul's letters where the phrase "the time had fully come" occurs, unless we take Paul to be the author of Ephesians (Eph. 1:10). It is a phrase that occurs in other parts of the NT in the context of speaking of the initiation of Christ's salvific work (e.g., Mark 1:15; John 7:8).

The word *exapostellō,* **sent,** indicates being sent on a commission. The cognate noun is "apostle."

**4:5** / The **law** must refer to the Torah, since Christ was born under it (4:4).

**4:6–7** / The ancient world thought of human **hearts** as that part of the human being that determined action, feeling, and thought. As J. Behm puts it, in the NT "the heart is the centre of the inner life of man and the source or seat of all forces and functions of soul and spirit" ("*kardia,*" *TDNT* 3:605–13, esp. p. 611). With the Spirit of God's Son in one's heart one's whole being may be transformed into a likeness to God's Son.

***Abba*** is a Greek transliteration of the Aramaic word for father. There were several words for father in the Jewish tradition. "Abba" was the form of familiar familial address of a son, often an adult son, to his human father. As J. Barr notes, the word "was not a childish expression comparable with 'Daddy': it was more a solemn, responsible, adult address to a Father" ("Abba Isn't 'Daddy,' " *JTS* 39 [1988], pp. 28–47, p. 46). Paul's reference to God as father appears to be the first time a Jewish writer refers to God in prayer as "Abba."

W. A. Meeks suggests that this verse reflects a baptismal setting. "The newly baptized person shouted out the Aramaic word *Abba* ('Father'), and . . . this was understood as the Spirit speaking through him, at the same time indicating his adoption as 'child of God' " (*The First Urban Christians: The Social World of the Apostle Paul* [New Haven: Yale University Press, 1983], p. 152; italics his). See also M. MacDonald, *The Pauline Churches: A Socio-Historical Study of Institutionalization in the Pauline and Deutero-Pauline Writings* (Cambridge: Cambridge University Press, 1988), p. 66.

## §17 A Reminder of What the Galatians Have Been Liberated From (Gal. 4:8–11)

**4:8** / After proclaiming what the Galatians are, Paul reminds them of what they were. In contrast to their present state, in which they **know God,** the Galatians' former life was one of slavery to **those who by nature are not gods.** This may recall Paul's evangelistic preaching, in which he brought them to a recognition of the one God. Implicit in this description is the contrast between slavery and freedom, which will become an increasingly prominent theme of the letter.

**4:9** / Paul again describes and contrasts the Galatians' present and former life. Reiterating that the Galatians **know God,** Paul further describes their present life as one of being **known by God.** A similar concept is expressed in 4:6–7, where Paul claims that the Galatians have been adopted by God and made heirs.

Stressing his incredulity that his readers might be willing to give up so much, Paul asks how they can think of **turning back.** His question reminds them that their desire to add law-observance brings them nothing new but only returns them to their former state of slavery. Pushing his point still further, Paul describes the **principles** as the worst kind of masters—**weak and miserable.** Instead of living in the freedom of children of the one God, the Galatians are being seduced into returning to the service of impotent and grasping masters. For Gentile believers the practice of Judaism is equivalent to their former life of servitude "to those who by nature are not gods."

**4:10** / The accusatory statement that the Galatians are **observing special days and months and seasons and years** uses the present tense, as does the previous question in verse 9, "do you wish to be enslaved . . . all over again?" While it is clear from 5:2–11 that the majority of the Galatian believers were not yet circumcised, there is nothing theoretical in Paul's current statement. Every indication in their behavior leads Paul to fear that his readers are close to taking the ultimate and irrevocable step of becoming circumcised.

It has been suggested that by "months" Paul may be referring to Jewish observance of monthly events, perhaps particularly events in the seventh month (Num. 29; also Num. 10:10; 28:11), and that by seasons Paul refers to Jewish festivals that went on for more than a day (so Burton, *Galatians,* pp. 233–34). However, it is difficult to fit Jewish cultic practices neatly into Paul's description of his readers' practice of observing special times. For one thing, Jewish time keeping referred to "festivals," not "seasons."

Honoring of seasons and cycles of the year was part of Celtic religion (A. M. Draak, "The Religion of the Celts," in *Historia Religionum* [ed. C. J. Bleeker and G. Widengren; vol. 1; Leiden: E. J. Brill, 1969], 629–46, esp. p. 644). Given that Paul is saying both that the Galatians are returning to serve the "basic principles" and that they are observing special times, the practice he describes in this verse is likely that of a return to former pagan religious customs, albeit interpreted and reshaped somewhat under the direction of the troublemakers. The rival evangelists may have been encouraging the Galatians to adopt the law on the basis of the principle that Jesus was the Messiah and that the inheritance of Abraham accrued only to law observers. They may also have favorably related the Galatians' previous pagan rituals with a law-observant life. The option of adding the law to their faith would then appear to the Galatians to be a return to a familiar way of living in the world, one in which the rhythms of the year were observed and celebrated. As Paul writes, he is aware that the Galatians have already given up part of the new way of living that was theirs in Christ and have begun to take on a self-identity more akin to their former paganism—one that feels beholden to the forces of the world and that, in pursuit of security, seeks a defining framework of religious observance.

**4:11** / Paul ends this part of his appeal with an expression of anxiety: **I fear for you, that somehow I have wasted my efforts on you.** Throughout the letter Paul has made his emotions plain: he has expressed astonishment (1:6), bewildered concern (3:1–5), and now fear. Paul uses all the resources at his disposal to convince the Galatians that they have all they need in Christ and that to take on law observance is to lose the new, free, and sufficient life into which they have entered.

## Additional Notes §17

**4:8** / This verse makes clear that the Galatians were pagans prior to conversion to Christ. Paul speaks of pagan gods in a similar way in 1 Cor. 8:5.

**4:10** / Cf. T. Martin, "Apostasy to Paganism: The Rhetorical Stasis of the Galatian Controversy," *JBL* 114/3 (1995), pp. 437–61; "Pagan and Judeo-Christian Time-Keeping Schemes in Gal. 4.10 and Col. 2.16," *NTS* 42 (1996), pp. 105–19, esp. pp. 113–19.

The word **observing** *(paratēresthe)* in connection with religious practice occurs only here in the NT. A similar use is found in Josephus, who speaks of Jews observing sabbath days (*Ant.* 3.91; 14.264).

**4:11** / Paul's concern for the Galatians themselves is evident from the fact that the word **you** is repeated twice.

## §18 An Appeal on the Basis of Friendship (Gal. 4:12–20)

**4:12** / Paul now works to convince the Galatians on the grounds of their being **brothers.** In the ancient world, as today, it was common to appeal to friendship as the basis upon which an action might be requested.

Paul chooses a different tack and commands his readers to **become like me.** He states that he **became like** them, by which statement he likely refers to the fact that, upon understanding that salvation came solely through Christ, he had become like a Gentile. Compare 2:14, where Paul describes Peter's life as like a Gentile, until the men from James arrived. Just as Paul rejected law observance to become as a Gentile, so he directs the Galatians to reject law observance and remain Gentiles. After the previous arguments from Scripture, experience, and reason Paul moves into a more personal vein with his readers, emphasizing his relationship with the Galatians in an attempt to dissuade them from turning to the law. This is not the first time that Paul has spoken personally, but 4:12–20 will be his most extensive appeal to the special bond he has shared with his converts. Paul recalls for his readers the fact that previously they did him **no wrong.** Paul wishes to cast their current course of action as a betrayal of the good beginning of their friendship.

**4:13–14** / Paul begins his retelling of the start of their friendship with **you know** (*oidate*), requiring the Galatians to consider their experience of him instead of the troublemakers' presentation of him. In the Greek Paul uses the word "flesh" (*sarx*) here and in the following verse (translated "illness," v. 14), thereby recalling for his readers his bodily presence with them.

Paul reminds them that they heard the gospel **because of an illness.** His original readers are the only ones who know precisely what illness Paul had, although 4:15 might indicate that it had something to do with Paul's sight. The Galatians were tempted to reject him and his gospel, but instead when he was present with them they **welcomed** him. In contrast to their current willingness in his absence to be persuaded away from his gospel, then they understood him to be **as an angel of God.**

Despite the trying nature of his illness, the Galatians **did not treat** him **with contempt or scorn,** as they are now doing. Paul's use of the strong words "contempt" and "scorn" indicates as much about how he sees the present state of his relationship with the Galatians as it does about the temptation the Galatians resisted on his original visit. Paul's claim that he was welcomed **as if** he **were Christ Jesus** vividly reminds the Galatians of the completeness of their conversion through his preaching. They knew in his gospel the presence of Christ.

**4:15** / In a poignant demand Paul asks his readers **what has happened to all** their **joy.** The word "joy" (*makarismos*) may be translated also "praise," "happiness," or "blessing." It is the word found in the Sermon on the Mount for "blessed." Paul is appealing to the Galatians' former attitude of goodwill toward him and to the blessing they experienced through their attachment to him. Their complete acceptance and care of Paul, in which they would even have **torn out** their **eyes and given them to** him, was the crucible in which they knew blessing.

**4:16** / Paul's next statement rests on the conviction that to oppose him is to oppose **the truth** and that his opponents are enemies of the truth (cf. 5:7). Paul equates the gospel with truth (2:5, 14) and understands his preaching and teaching, both now and in the past, as truth telling. If he is now regarded as an **enemy** it is not because his message was wrong. The implication is clear—what is false is the portrait of him created by the rival evangelists.

**4:17** / And Paul in turn paints a negative image of his opponents. They court the favor of the Galatians **for no good.** Unlike he himself, who invited the Galatians into the truth of the gospel, Paul charges that the troublemakers want **to alienate** the Galatians. The Greek does not make explicit from what the Galatians might be alienated. The NIV translation interprets this verse as Paul saying that his opponents want to alienate his converts "from us," that is, from Paul and "all the brothers with me" (1:2). As a few verses later Paul expresses anguish over whether or not Christ is being formed in his converts (v. 19), in all likelihood Paul is saying that his rivals are seeking to alienate the Galatians from being "in Christ" (cf. 5:4). A little later Paul expresses anguish over whether or not Christ is being formed in his converts (v. 19). Whatever his precise meaning, Paul is saying that the agitators' motives are to separate the Galatian churches from what is good and life-giving.

Paul says that the troublemakers are courting the Galatians simply for their own ends—**so that you may be zealous for them.** From the vantage point of hundreds of years later it is impossible to tell exactly what this means. But the general criticism Paul makes is plain enough. The rival evangelists are cultivating a following among the Galatians for their own advantage.

Paul sees the situation somewhat as would a jilted lover— he and the Galatians had a good and devoted relationship and now a rival is making promises that in the lover's eyes can only damage his beloved. Paul sees his opponents as malicious troublemakers who will lead the Galatians to damnation.

**4:18** / It is not the rival evangelists' zealousness for the Galatians that Paul thinks is wrong. The problem is that their zealousness is not for a **purpose** that **is good.** Paul subtly encourages the Galatians to recognize that through his letter he too is making much of them for a good purpose. Paul encourages the Galatians to turn their attention to cultivating *his* favor instead of that of the troublemakers.

**4:19** / Paul describes the character and quality of his commitment to the Galatians. He portrays his concern and his role with them, using the powerful image of giving birth. This is the first time that Paul has spoken of the Galatians as his **dear children,** and it introduces a passage in which he will focus on children (4:25, 27, 28, 31).

Paul thinks the Galatians are so dangerously close to being lost from Christ that he is **again in the pains of childbirth.** He gave them their new life through preaching the gospel that gives life (cf. 3:21). And now he is once more in the position of giving himself entirely to the good purpose of having **Christ** be **formed** in them. Paul's expression conveys confidence that this purpose will be accomplished.

Although this is the only place Paul uses the phrase "Christ is formed in you," it encapsulates the basic vision of Paul's gospel. In 2 Corinthians 3:18 the apostle puts it this way: "being transformed into his likeness with ever-increasing glory." Romans

8:29 also contains the idea of being conformed to Christ (cf. Phil. 3:10, which speaks of being conformed to Christ's death).

**4:20** / Paul closes this section on a conciliatory note: he wishes he **could be with** them **now** so that he **could change** his **tone.** Unlike his relationship with some of his other churches (e.g., 2 Cor. 10:10), Paul thinks that his physical presence with the Galatian churches could make a difference in their behavior. At the moment he is uncertain about them, but if he were physically with them he might be able to stop being **perplexed.**

---

### Additional Notes §18

---

**4:13** / The **first** that he **preached the gospel** can mean either "the first time," indicating there was more than one visit, or "at one time, formerly," which does not necessarily indicate more than one visit. When the Greek *to proteron* is translated as a comparative adjective meaning "first" it indicates that Paul has subsequently visited the Galatians. Scholars seeking to determine the destination and date of Galatians on the basis of the Acts narrative ask whether the first visit refers to Paul's initial contacts with those in south Galatia (Acts 13:14–14:20) or north Galatia (Acts 16:6). See the Introduction for more on this.

**4:14** / The term **angel of God** is found in the story of Hagar (Gen. 21:17), a story to which Paul will subsequently turn. Throughout Galatians, Paul has presented himself as the one who can speak truly on God's behalf. Such a self-understanding is found throughout his letters (e.g., 2 Cor. 5:20).

**4:17** / The proposal of R. Jewett goes a long way toward providing a plausible historical occasion for Paul's words. Jewett suggests that the increase in Jewish nationalism in Palestine in the period of Paul's writing Galatians meant that all Jews who had contacts with Gentiles were in danger of persecution from other Jews; the agenda of the troublemakers was in part to protect Jewish members of the church, particularly those in Judea who were known to have connection to Gentiles throughout the Mediterranean world. If the troublemakers could achieve the circumcision of Gentiles who had contact with Jews they would protect Judean Jewish Christians and gain "public recognition for their loyalty to Torah" ("The Agitators and the Galatian Congregation," *NTS* 17 [1971], pp. 198–212, esp. p. 206). This proposal may also explain 6:12. For a critique of Jewett see Murphy-O'Connor, *Paul: A Critical Life*, pp. 140–41.

**4:19** / Paul is given to parental images for his relationship with his converts (e.g., 1 Cor. 4:14–15). The image of **childbirth** is startling for the man Paul, although he does use other maternal images (e.g., 1 Cor. 3:1–4; 1 Thess. 2:7). The imagery of childbirth was used in ancient Jewish literature to describe the birthing of a new age, the radical transition from this aeon to the next. In the prophets the day of the Lord is spoken of using the metaphor of a woman giving birth (Mic. 4:10; Isa. 13:6, 8; Jer. 6:24). We find a similar imagery in *1 Enoch* 62:4; *2 Baruch* 56:6; *4 Ezra* 4:42; and in the non-Pauline NT (e.g., Mark 13:8). As B. Gaventa writes: "We find in these texts an established association between apocalyptic expectation and the anguish of childbirth" ("The Maternity of Paul: An Exegetical Study of Galatians 4:19," in *The Conversation Continues: Studies in Paul and John* [Nashville: Abingdon, 1990], pp. 189–201, 193). In Romans Paul uses the metaphor in a similar way (8:22–23). Since Paul has claimed that his gospel concerns "the one who gave himself for our sins to rescue us from the present evil age" (1:4), his reference to giving birth suggests that he regarded himself as a divinely appointed agent in this transfer of the ages.

**4:20** / Betz writes:

> Paul had started out in 3:1 by addressing the Galatians as "simpletons." . . . So far, chapters 3 and 4 contained heavy argumentative and deeply felt emotional sections. The arguments all went overwhelmingly in favor of the Apostle. According to the psychology of ancient rhetoric, however, people who are to be persuaded should not be left in such a low situation. By confessing his own perplexity in 4:20 Paul removes himself from the haughty position of one who has all the arguments and all the answers. (*Galatians*, p. 237)

Paul's wish to be present with his readers is a standard feature of his letters (e.g., Rom. 1:11; 1 Thess. 2:17–18; 3:6, 10; 1 Cor. 16:7). See T. Y. Mullins, "Visit Talk in New Testament Letters," *CBQ* 35 (1973), pp. 350–58. Reference to such a desire was the way Paul and other ancient letter writers expressed their care for the addressees.

## §19 Paul's Interpretation of the Scripture Used by the Rival Evangelists (Gal. 4:21–5:1)

**4:21** / Paul's tone changes somewhat at this point, turning from a personal appeal back to an argument from Scripture (cf. 3:6–9) and to teaching what he and the Galatian believers already have in Christ. Paul begins with a direct address, **Tell me, you who want to be under the law.** The wording of the question critiques their desire, for Paul presents the law as something under which people are held.

The passage beginning in this verse and extending to 5:1 works with several themes that have already been introduced: giving birth (3:19), slavery (3:8), freedom (3:25), Abraham (3:6–8, 16–18, 29), the promise (3:14, 18, 21–22, 29), sonship (4:5–7), a covenant (cf. 3:15), persecution of believers in Christ by Jews (1:13), and inheritance (3:18; 4:1–7).

Themes and features from Genesis 21 appear in Galatians 4:21–5:1—Abraham, Abraham's wife, Hagar, the two sons, promise, inheritance, and the quotation from Genesis 21:10. Other themes from the Genesis text appear in the rest of the letter—circumcision, the legitimate offspring. The fact that Paul has worked indirectly with Genesis 21 throughout the letter and now deals with it head on suggests that it has been a key text for the circumcisers' argument. The Galatians were Gentiles and so would not have known much of the Jewish writings unless they had been taught them in the context of their new religion. That Genesis 21 is so central to the letter, both implicitly and explicitly, suggests that Paul feels constrained to respond to an interpretation of it being promulgated by the rival evangelists.

The twice-repeated phrase "for it is written" (vv. 22, 27) and the question "but what does the Scripture say?" (v. 30) indicate that now Paul takes his primary task to be scriptural interpretation. He faces the challenge of undoing the rival evangelists' interpretation of the passage, which most likely made more plain sense than the one he presents. This may be why he

speaks of his interpretation as figurative (4:24). The rival evangelists could point to Genesis 21 in support of their argument that
inheriting the promise of Abraham entailed circumcision. Only
Isaac, the circumcised son, carries on Abraham's line.

**4:22–23** / Paul launches into an interpretation of the
scriptural passage that the troublemakers had been using to pro-
mote their cause. He begins by noting that **Abraham had two
sons** and that the difference between these two sons is that **one**
was **by the slave woman and the other by the free woman.** He
then moves to his figurative interpretation by explaining that the
**son by the slave woman was born in the ordinary way; but his
son by the free woman was born as the result of a promise.** In
the Greek the phrase "born in the ordinary way" is "born according to the flesh *(sarx).*" While the Genesis text does understand
Isaac to be the child of God's promise (Gen. 21:1–3) Paul's description of Ishmael as "born according to the flesh" goes beyond
contrasting Isaac's special birth with the normal birth of Ishmael.
In the context of this passage, which uses dualistic categories,
Paul's use of "flesh" puts a particular slant on the story, casting
the rivalry between Sarah and Hagar and Isaac and Ishmael in
terms of the enmity between the promise or the Spirit (cf. 3:14)
and the flesh, which is opposed to the Spirit (see esp. 5:16–25).

Paul's reference to "promise" alludes to a concept that he
and his readers agree is a good thing. The Galatians wish to be assured of receiving the promise of Abraham, and Paul builds a
case that his gospel has secured the promise.

**4:24–25** / Paul takes the allegory further by speaking of
the two **women** as **two covenants.** This clearly goes well beyond
Genesis, but Paul has admitted that he speaks **figuratively.** He
equates **Hagar** with **Mount Sinai.** In doing so he also says that
this covenant **bears children who are to be slaves,** emphasizing
this by stating that Mount Sinai is **in Arabia,** the land in which
Ishmael, the child of the slave woman, settled (Gen. 26:18).
Whereas Judaism stresses the privilege that comes from the law,
Paul here uses the Jewish Scriptures to say the opposite: the Jewish covenant enslaves. Going on with his allegory, Paul states
that there is a correspondence between Hagar (i.e., Mount Sinai)
and **the present city of Jerusalem,** a city **in slavery with her children.** The word **corresponds** *(systoicheō)* is built on the same
root as the word translated "basic principles" in 4:3 and 9. It
means "stand in the same line." Paul's point is that the Galatian

congregation chose the wrong line to stand in when they agreed to be influenced by the present Jerusalem.

In Galatians the word **covenant** appears only here and in Paul's illustration in Galatians 3:15–17. The word is especially fitting in the context of dealing with the Abraham tradition, for in the Septuagint the same word appears in the story of God establishing his covenant with Abraham and requiring from Abraham circumcision (Gen. 17:7–14).

Paul's statement concerning two covenants would have been shocking to Jewish sensibilities. First, while the Jewish tradition held that God had made several covenants with Israel, among them the covenant with Noah, the covenant with Abraham, the covenant with Moses, covenants with Josiah and Nehemiah, the covenant with David, and the promise of a new covenant (Jer. 31:31–4; see also Rom. 9:4, which has the word "covenant" in the plural), these events were understood within the broad category of the Jewish religion as a religion of the covenant. In Judaism there was one covenant, just as for Paul there was only one gospel. Second, Paul argues that there is a covenant that does not require circumcision. For Jews the word covenant was almost synonymous with circumcision (see particularly Gen. 17:10).

**4:26** / The name and symbol of **Jerusalem** appear to have had a strategic position in the rhetoric of the rival evangelists and of Paul (see esp. 1:13–2:21). The troublemakers were no doubt claiming that the authority of the Jerusalem church stood behind their gospel. Paul is willing to concede that his opponents may have the present Jerusalem on their side, but he asserts that he too can claim the backing of Jerusalem—**the** Jerusalem **that is above,** that **is free,** that **is our mother.**

Paul assures his readers that they already have all they need through faith in Christ when he supplements the metaphor of a son inheriting the father's will with the image of the "Jerusalem above" as the mother of believers. The statement is a simple declarative one in which Paul states what he considers to be a fact: his converts have been born from the free woman, which is to say that they are the ones "born as the result of a promise" (4:23). It follows that the Galatians should stop seeking the promise through the present Jerusalem, which can offer only the inheritance of slavery (cf. 4:24–5).

**4:27** / Paul supports his interpretation with a quotation from the Septuagint of Isaiah 54:1. Even though in Genesis it is

Hagar, not Sarah, who is unmarried, Sarah is the referent for the **barren woman.** The "Jerusalem above" who is "our mother" is also a reference to Sarah (v. 26).

The quotation uses the imperative mood, commanding the "barren woman" to **break forth and cry aloud.** As Paul has just stated that he and his converts share the Jerusalem above as their mother (4:26), he may be using this text to encourage his readers to recognize and participate in rejoicing over the miraculous birth that is theirs. The underlying theme of who is a legitimate child, which has surfaced at various places in the letter (e.g., 3:29–4:7), is again in evidence. While the agitators may be characterizing the Galatians' mother as unmarried and the Galatians as illegitimate children, Paul is saying that their mother has received her promise of numerous children, and they should see themselves as part of the fulfillment of that promise.

Since Paul has earlier spoken of himself as birthing the Galatians (4:19), he may be employing the quotation from Isaiah to refer also to himself. He is shouting forth that his children are the children of the promise.

**4:28** / Paul states his meaning plainly. The allegorical utterance of Scripture can be applied directly to the Galatians: they, **like Isaac, are children of promise.** Paul's interpretive boldness in declaring that his uncircumcised converts are kin to Isaac, who was circumcised on the eight day (Gen. 21:4), is in line with his conviction that his gospel and his converts manifest the fulfillment of God's promise to Abraham.

**4:29** / Continuing to apply the scriptural story to the current situation—**it is the same now**—Paul makes the point that Ishmael **(the son born in the ordinary way) persecuted** Isaac **(the son born by the power of the Spirit).** The contrast of the child born in the ordinary way and the one born by the power of the Spirit resonates with the contrast Paul set up in 4:23, although there the second child was "born as the result of a promise."

The Genesis story contains no reference to Ishmael persecuting Isaac or to the Spirit, but Paul is applying the text of Scripture to the text of life. Having identified his readers with Isaac, he maintains that they are being persecuted by Ishmael, who in Paul's mind likely corresponds primarily to the Jewish Christian troublemakers and perhaps secondarily to Jews in general (4:24–5). As is clear from 4:17, Paul understands the influence of the rival evangelists on his converts as a form of harassment.

Paul sets up a parallelism here with the previous statement, so that "children of promise" are equated with the son born "according to the power of the Spirit." This is typical of the correspondence Paul makes throughout the letter between the promise and the Spirit (e.g., 3:14). In the remainder of Galatians the focus will shift from the promise to an increasing attention on the Spirit.

**4:30** / Paul cites Sarah's expression of distress over whether Ishmael might be included in the inheritance (Gen. 21:10). As Paul has made it plain that he is using the Scripture in direct reference to the Galatians' own circumstances, his question **what does the Scripture say?** implicitly includes the words "to us." Paul takes Sarah's command that Hagar and Ishmael be driven out as a command on target for the Galatians. The **inheritance** belongs to his converts, and it shall not be shared with those who preach a different gospel.

The quotation dramatizes the choice before the Galatians. Through association with the rival evangelists Paul's converts are identified with Hagar and Ishmael, which means they are the ones driven out and excluded from Abraham's inheritance.

**4:31** / In order to be sure his readers understand, Paul declares **we are not children of the slave woman, but of the free woman.** Like Isaac, the Galatians are Abraham's heirs. The troublemakers were undoubtedly suggesting that unless Paul's Gentile converts followed the law they were not part of the people of God, but Paul says the opposite.

**5:1** / The means by which the Gentile Galatians have become children of the free woman is through **Christ.** This is another way of saying what Paul said earlier—that "Christ redeemed us from the curse of the law" (3:13). Paul declares that the purpose of Christ's work was **for freedom.** The concept of freedom, which is a basic theme of Galatians, is connected throughout Paul's letters primarily with freedom *from:* freedom from the law (Rom. 7:3–4), from sin (Rom. 6:18–22), or from death (Rom. 8:2). Freedom is also equated with the Spirit (2 Cor. 3:17) and is used as a way to describe the Christian life (Gal. 2:4). In an expansive command, Paul directs his readers to **stand firm** against the influence of the rival evangelists. Underscoring the point he has made repeatedly, Paul charges his converts not to put themselves in a position of submitting to **a yoke of slavery**. To such a fate, Paul warns, his readers' attraction to the alternative gospel leads.

Throughout the letter Paul has described the adding of law to faith and the Galatians' former life (4:8–9) as enslavement, which is why he can warn that the Galatians' attraction to the rival evangelists' message will mean that they are slaves once **again**.

---

### Additional Notes §19

---

**4:21** / See A. T. Lincoln, who notes that this Scripture "is being used by [Paul's] opponents to their own advantage" (*Paradise Now and Not Yet: Studies in the Role of the Heavenly Dimension in Paul's Thought With Special Reference to His Eschatology* [Cambridge: Cambridge University Press, 1981], p. 12). See also C. K. Barrett, "The Allegory of Abraham, Sarah and Hagar in the Argument of Galatians," in *Rechtfertigung: Festschrift für Ernst Käsemann zum 70. Geburtstag* (ed. J. Friedrich, W. Pöhlmann, and P. Stuhlmacher [Tübingen: J. C. B. Mohr {Paul Siebeck}, 1976]), pp. 1–16.

**4:24** / The word **figuratively** is the translation of the compound Greek word *allēgoroumena*, which means "say something else" and is often translated as "allegory." The Greek form is participial and might best be translated "allegorical sayings." In the Greco-Roman world a respected way to interpret sacred or ancient tradition was to regard its sayings as allegorical, that is, as referring to something not immediately evident from the text itself. Philo used allegory extensively. The following rabbinical saying describes the interpretive mind-set that employs allegory: "As the hammer causes many sparks to fly, so the word of Scripture has a manifold sense" (in the Babylonian Talmud, *Sanhedrin* 34a; quoted from F. Büschsel, "*allēgoreō*," *TDNT* 1:260–64, esp. p. 263). Paul demonstrates an allegorical interpretive approach elsewhere in his letters (e.g., 1 Cor. 9:8–10; 10:1–11), although nowhere else does he designate his interpretation an allegory.

**4:25** / The statement **Hagar stands for Mount Sinai in Arabia** has several variant readings in the manuscripts, among the most important being those which leave out the name "Hagar" and read simply, "For Sinai is a mountain in Arabia." The NIV's reading is the more difficult one and so more likely original. Some scholars have attempted to explain Paul's meaning by pointing out that the Hebrew word for Hagar has similarities to an Arabic word meaning rock and so have suggested that here Paul is saying "Hagar means mountain in Arabia." Paul has, however, stated that he is approaching the whole issue figuratively, and so there is no need to make his interpretation more straightforward than he himself felt the need to do.

Arabia is not only the place associated in the Genesis narrative with the descendants of Ishmael (Gen. 25:18) but also the place Paul went after his call and conversion (Gal. 1:17).

The antecedent of the pronoun "her" in the phrase **her children** refers to Jerusalem and to Hagar, the meaning being "Jerusalem, like Hagar, is in slavery with her children" (Longenecker, *Galatians*, p. 213).

**4:26** / The concept of **Jerusalem that is above** was not unfamiliar to Judaism. Ezekiel is given a vision of a heavenly Jerusalem that would be the model for the new Jerusalem to be built (Ezek. 40–48). But, while there is precedence in Jewish literature for the concept of a heavenly Jerusalem, such a Jerusalem was thought to be a counterpart to the earthly Jerusalem. Paul's contrasting of the present with the heavenly Jerusalem appears to be unique (see Lincoln, *Paradise Now and Not Yet*, pp. 18–22).

The Jerusalem that is above has a future and a present referent. It is to be understood within the context of hope (vv. 27–28; see W. Horbury, "Land, Sanctuary and Worship," in *Early Christian Thought in Its Jewish Context* [ed. J. Barclay and J. Sweet; Cambridge: Cambridge University Press, 1996], pp. 207–24) and of present reality (v. 26; "she *is* our mother"). Paul's claim that the heavenly Jerusalem is now present resides, as Lincoln has noted, within the apocalyptic framework. Lincoln comments, "as in the apocalyptic and Qumran references what is to be revealed at the end can be thought of as already existing" (*Paradise Now and Not Yet*, p. 21). Such a claim on Paul's part corresponds to his affirmation that Christ's death delivered believers "from the present evil age" (1:4). Paul is working with apocalyptic categories (see Isa. 65:17–25) and framing the life of believers within the birth of the new age: a moment in time in which the present and future are uniquely conjoined.

The Jewish Scriptures could refer to Jerusalem as a **mother** (e.g., Isa. 49:14–15; 51:18; Ps. 87:5; cf. 2 Esdras 10:7), as is demonstrated in Paul's citation from Isaiah (54:1) in the following verse.

**4:27** / The Greek term **barren woman** in Isa. 54:1 [LXX] is found also in Gen. 11:30 [LXX], where it refers to Sarah. This particular text was used in Jewish writings that spoke of eschatological hopes (see *Targum Isaiah* on 54:1) for a restored Jerusalem.

**4:29** / While no OT Scripture describes Ishmael persecuting Isaac, the Hebrew word for "playing" in Gen. 21:9 could also denote "mocking." On the basis of this meaning later Jewish interpretive writings contain stories of Ishmael harassing Isaac. See Longenecker (*Galatians*, pp. 200–206) for rabbinic references.

**4:30** / The words "free woman" are not found in the Septuagint version of Gen. 21:10. Paul appears to have added them so as to clarify his application of the text.

## §20 Paul's Direct Warning: To Become Circumcised Is to Be Divorced from Christ (Gal. 5:2–6)

**5:2** / Now Paul turns up the heat with a direct address— **Mark my words! I, Paul, tell you.** No longer using Scripture, Paul states forthrightly: **if you let yourselves be circumcised, Christ will be of no value to you at all.** The options are clearly laid out: either circumcision without Christ or Christ without circumcision. While Paul has referred to the "circumcision group" (2:12) as those who are opposed to the "truth of the gospel" and has particularly through the references to Abraham alluded to circumcision as a divisive concern in the Galatian congregation, this is the first time he has named the issue and tackled it.

Paul's warning not to be circumcised reads in the Greek as something that the Galatians are tempted to do but have not yet done. The sign of circumcision was equated with being a Jew (cf. 2:7–8). Therefore Paul considers that in the context of belief in Christ, circumcision bears a different meaning depending on whether or not one came into the faith already circumcised. If one was already a Jew, then circumcision counted for nothing (cf. 5:6). It should be the same for Gentiles. Paul clearly accepted that circumcised Jews were part of the faith (2:7–8), but he would not accept that a Gentile believer could receive circumcision and remain in Christ. To become circumcised after faith in Christ is to accord significance to circumcision and so to deny Christ.

**5:3** / Paul testifies **again ... to every man who lets himself be circumcised that he is obligated to obey the whole law.** To be circumcised after conversion to Christ was to add the law and deny the sufficiency of Christ (cf. 2:21). Paul is confident that if Gentile believers enter Judaism through circumcision they will discover that they have lost the unfurled life that is now theirs in

Christ. They will find themselves operating within a different
and less satisfactory worldview.

It is noteworthy that Paul does not say to his readers that
he left law observance because he found it ineffective. He asserts
that already he and they have through Christ all that could ever
be hoped for. To add law is to change the focus of their life and
so lose.

**5:4** / Paul reduces the situation to its essentials. Charg-
ing that the intention of those contemplating circumcision is
that they are **trying to be justified by law,** Paul says that this
means they no longer have Christ. By turning to law, they are at-
tempting to receive from the law what they already have in
Christ—righteousness—and so they effectively cut themselves
off **from Christ** (cf. 4:19). The choice is the Galatians' to make.
They are in Christ and in God's grace as they are. They will not
lose the benefit of Christ through remaining as Gentiles, as the
agitators are asserting. But if they choose to adopt law they will
fall **from grace,** for they will have chosen to refuse God's gift of
Christ's self-offering (cf. 2:21, "if justification comes through the
law, then Christ died for nothing"). In the face of the Galatians'
fascination with the law Paul has repeatedly argued that justification comes through Christ and faith, not law (2:16, 21; 3:6, 8,
11, 21, 24).

The parallelism in which Paul places Christ and grace resonates with the opening of the letter, where Paul spoke of his gospel as "the grace of Christ" (1:6). Grace is a central way to explain
God's response to and relationship with humanity. God gives
freely and Paul's gospel is a witness to the grace (gift) of God in
Christ's death (Gal. 2:21).

**5:5** / Paul distinguishes the path the Galatians are considering from the one they are on. As believers they live in hope
of righteousness, a hope that is theirs **by faith . . . through the
Spirit.** Paul brings together several strands of his argument: the
Spirit, which is the evidence that the promise made to Abraham
is given to Gentiles (3:14), is the means by which righteousness is
given; righteousness is given to those of faith (2:16; 3:6–9), who
are those who have received the Spirit (3:2). But, perhaps in recognition of the Galatians' legitimate and realistic recognition
that they do not yet display the traits of righteous people, Paul
also nuances his case. He speaks of **the righteousness for which
we hope,** in contrast to his earlier statement that believers are

justified through the faith of Christ (2:16). In this he possibly demonstrates respect for the Galatians' concern that their faith in Christ has not yet made them righteous. After all, the Galatian Christians would not have been attracted to law observance unless they had felt some deficiency in their Christian lives. In response Paul declares that his converts can expect righteousness only through his gospel, which is why they and he may now wait **eagerly.** The outcome is assured for those "in Christ."

The phrase "the righteousness for which we hope" can be taken to mean either hope that has righteousness as its object or hope that righteousness produces. Commentators are divided over this matter, depending on whether or not they want to harmonize this phrase with statements in the letter that present righteousness as a present state for believers. For those who think Paul is consistent on this issue the second option is chosen (so Matera, *Galatians*, p. 182). The first option is the choice of those who think that since righteousness refers both to behavior and standing before God, there is an "already–not yet" aspect to Paul's view of righteousness for believers (e.g., Burton, *Galatians*, p. 278). It is also possible that even in those places where Paul is usually interpreted as saying that righteousness is a present reality (2:16 and 3:21), he may be speaking of righteousness as a dynamic state that has begun and will continue to grow. Paul's subsequent advice about the character of living by the Spirit (5:16) would suggest that he understands righteousness as the new reality into which believers have been transferred and by which they now are being shaped.

**5:6** / **In Christ . . . neither circumcision nor uncircumcision has any value.** The shape of the believer's life is defined by being in Christ, which is what Paul affirmed earlier in 3:28. The power the believer has is the power of faith, which is effective **through love.** Paul sets in semantic parallelism being "in Christ" and "faith working through love." This is another way of saying that it is the faith of Christ that justifies (2:16; see Introduction). As believers share in Christ's faith, so they share in his love (cf. 2:20). Believers put on Christ (3:27) and so become as Christ, the one who is the epitome of faith working through love.

The phrase "faith expressing itself through love" can also be translated "faith made effective through love," depending on whether the Greek verb "expressing" (*energoumenē*) is read as a middle or a passive; "made effective" is the middle form. Since Paul has used this word with the middle sense in Galatians 2:8 and 3:5, it is likely that here it also has that meaning. The verse would then mean that faith comes to expression by means of love. This points to what Paul has said elsewhere: Christ is the one who loves (2:20), and believers in Christ become as Christ (3:27) through participating in the faith of Christ (2:16). For Galatian believers concerned about righteousness and willing to turn to the law as a guarantee this statement hits the mark. Paul states that faith is not abstract but a way of life that is made effective, visibly and daily, through love. Paul has in view the love of Christ in which believers participate through being "in Christ." This love will be manifest in love of neighbor (5:13).

---

## Additional Notes §20

---

**5:2** / It is rare for **Paul** to use his name within a letter. Usually his name occurs only in the opening and sometimes at the closing of his letters.

**5:3** / The word **declare**, *marturomai*, could also be translated "protest."

Both the rabbis and later Christians regarded circumcision as the step that obliged one to obey the entire law. The rabbis say: "A proselyte who accepts all commandments of the Tora except for one is not accepted; R. Yose son of Rabbi Yehuda says: even (if it concerns) a detail of the niceties of the Scribes." (*t. Demai* 2.5; quoted from P. J. Tomson, *Paul and the Jewish Law: Halakha in the Letters of the Apostle to the Gentiles* [Minneapolis: Fortress, 1990], pp. 88–89). Justin Martyr continues Paul's understanding that circumcision entails obeying the whole law (*Dial.* 8 [*ANF* 1.198–99]).

**5:4** / The words **alienated** (*katērgēthēte*) and **have fallen away** (*exepesate*) appear in the Greek in the aorist tense. Some scholars read this as a statement of what has already happened in the Galatian congregation (e.g., Burton, *Galatians*, p. 276; Betz, *Galatians*, p. 261; Longenecker, *Galatians*, p. 228). Others take the aorist in a proleptic sense (so Matera, *Galatians*, p. 182; Bruce, *Galatians*, p. 230); M. Zerwick writes: "the relative clause has a conditional sense 'if you seek justification in the law' and the aorist as it were dramatically represents the consequence as a historical fact, so as to insist the more on the imminence of the danger run by those who are being warned" (*Biblical Greek* [Rome: Pontifical Biblical Institute, 1990], para. 257). Perhaps Paul's aorist usage has both a past and a proleptic sense. Paul charges that his readers have already discounted grace through their temptation to follow the law, but the fact that he still feels it is worth his while to try to dissuade them means that hope remains.

**5:5** / In Greek the word **righteousness** is the same as the word "justified" in v. 4—*dikaiosynē*.

**5:6** / The Greek phrase *ti ischuei oute* translated **neither . . . has any value** conveys the sense "there is no strength."

## §21 Paul, Not the Rival Evangelists, Is on the Galatians' Side (Gal. 5:7–12)

**5:7** / Paul now changes his tactic somewhat and begins to use an approach common to persuasive speech—friendship through shared antipathy. Paul places himself and the Galatians in one camp against an opposition seeking to separate the Galatians from their goal. Paul affirms that in the past his readers were heading toward the goal in exemplary fashion—**you were running a good race.** They had been **obeying the truth.** The sense conveyed by the word "obey" is of having accepted a way of life and been willing to be shaped by it. But someone has stepped into their path and driven them off course—**who cut in on you?** Paul uses both singular (5:10) and plural (5:12; cf. 1:7) to refer to his opponents and never names them.

Paul uses the athletic imagery of running for living the Christian life (see also Gal. 2:2; Rom. 9:16; 1 Cor. 9:24–27; Phil. 2:16; 3:14; 2 Thess. 3:1). Athletic imagery was used frequently also in the ancient philosophers and expressed the idea of intense focus on the goal of the philosophical life. Philo speaks of "athletes of virtue" (*Good Person* 13.88 [Colson, LCL]). The image continues in Christian discourse. John Chrysostom speaks of raising Christian children as "rearing . . . athletes for [God]" (*On Vainglory and the Upbringing of Children* 90; quoted from M. Wiles and M. Santer, eds., *Documents in Early Christian Thought* [Cambridge: Cambridge University Press, 1975], p. 223).

The tense of the verb "cut in" (*enekopsen*) is aorist, which expresses a past action. As he indicated in 4:19, so here Paul considers that the Galatians have lost ground with Christ. Burton writes: "That Paul uses the aorist (resultative) rather than the present (conative) indicates that he is thinking of what his opponents have already accomplished in their obstructive work" (*Galatians*, p. 282).

This is the first time Paul has spoken of the truth as something to be obeyed, although he has elsewhere equated the gospel with the truth (2:5, 14) and his preaching as truth telling (4:16). Paul has presented himself as one who obeys God (in 1:10a the NIV translates "obey" as "win . . . approval").

**5:8** / Contrasting their previous obedience to the truth with the **persuasion** by which they are now being affected, Paul clarifies that God, **the one who calls** (cf. 1:6), is not the source of the influence the Galatians are experiencing. With the image of the race in the background, Paul is saying that his converts are now off course, following the wrong call.

**5:9** / The saying **"a little yeast works through the whole batch of dough"** is found also at 1 Corinthians 5:6. It appears to have been common in the ancient Greek-speaking world to use yeast as a symbol for evil's powerful corrupting capacity (cf. Mark 8:15). In this case Paul is warning that even though there may be only a few advocating circumcision their influence could damage the nature of the Galatian churches.

**5:10** / Even though throughout most of the letter it is clear that Paul doubts his Galatian readers' good sense, here he appeals to it in an attempt to encourage them to trust him and his gospel. Paul writes that he is **confident in the Lord that** they **take no other view** than the one he is presenting. Continuing to place himself alongside his readers, Paul depicts them as under the influence of a confuser (cf. 1:7).

The phrase **in the Lord** occurs frequently in Paul's letters, along with the phrase "in Christ." Paul sees himself as living in the Lord, in Christ. He reminds the Galatians that this is the basis of his confidence. The inference is that those who are contending for the Galatians' confidence are not in the Lord (cf. 5:8).

With the same confidence, Paul declares that the one confusing them **will pay the penalty.** This is another way for him to assert that he and his gospel are on God's side. Those who present an alternate gospel stand under the judgment of God. Paul assures his converts that if they do as he suggests everything will work out well and the troubles will pass.

**5:11** / After implicitly asking his readers to trust him because he trusts them, Paul must clear up any grounds for their mistrust of him. He responds to rumor—probably stemming from the "confusers"—that he has been **preaching circumcision**— by pointing out the ludicrousness of such a rumor. If he were preaching circumcision he would not be **being persecuted.**

Identifying his gospel here, as elsewhere, with the cross, Paul argues that his difficult position arises from the fact that he does not preach circumcision but **the offense of the cross.** Paul's message was that a human named Jesus, who was humble, obedient, and accepting of death on a cross, had been raised by God and now was the one before whom "every knee should bend, in heaven and on earth and under the earth, and every tongue should confess that Jesus Christ is Lord, to the glory of God the Father" (Phil. 2:10–11). Such a message was absurd to people in general (cf. 1 Cor. 1:18) and was scandalous to Jews. Yet the cross was the defining moment in God's salvific dealings with humanity. Paul says this another way in 2:21: "if justification could be gained through the law, Christ died for nothing." If he were to advocate circumcision for Gentiles he would be nullifying the death of Christ. Paul asks the Galatians, his **brothers,** to consider how preposterous such a thought is.

As he does elsewhere, Paul takes opportunity to defend himself against any lurking accusations about his credibility and to express boldly the radical position in which he stands. He is one whose proclamation brings him persecution. Paul's uncomfortable position in the world is confirmation of the truth of his message and the integrity of his life.

Acts states that the Jews persecuted Paul (e.g., Acts 26:21). Paul himself mentions the Jews as his persecutors (2 Cor. 11:24). The gospel would have been abhorrent to Jews, as it had been to Paul (Gal. 1:13; Phil. 3:6). Paul also includes other "servants of Christ" (2 Cor. 11:23) among his adversaries. On account of his law-free gospel for Gentiles, he experienced active opposition from some Jewish Christians. It behooved Jewish Christians to advocate circumcision so that they could interact with Gentile Christians without risk of being persecuted themselves (6:12; see notes on 4:17 and cf. Phil. 3:2–3). Paul may be including in his reference to persecution the fact that his cherished Galatian churches are being negatively influenced by the rival evangelists.

Paul regarded the cross as the pivotal point of his message and so as synonymous with the gospel (cf. 1 Cor. 1:17). The "message of the cross" is the saving power of God (1 Cor. 1:18), and thus those who oppose the gospel are "enemies of the cross of Christ" (Phil. 3:18). This identification of his gospel with the cross was a scandalous move, for the cross signified for the ancients the punishment due to the worst of society's offenders. Even the modern symbol of the electric chair does not match what Justin

Martyr calls the "despised and shameful mystery of the cross" *(Dial.* 131 [*ANF* 1.265]).

**5:12** / Confident that he has his readers on his side at last, Paul expresses the outrageous wish that the rival evangelists would let the knife slip on themselves. It is a darkly brilliant sentiment, showing that just as the result of his gospel is freedom, the result of his opponents' is the worst form of impotence. Paul plays with a concept similar to the one he used in 4:9, where he describes the life to which the Galatians were being attracted as akin to their former life of slavery to impotent and grasping masters. According to Deuteronomy 23:1 any male whose penis is cut off shall not be admitted to the assembly of the Lord. Paul's wish that the rival evangelists **emasculate themselves** may then also include a wish for a graphic demonstration that their message is alienated from God's plan.

Paul's use of the designation **agitators** for his rivals betrays more of his negative regard for them. This term is used elsewhere in the NT to signify political agitation (Acts 17:6; 21:38). Paul may be tarring his opponents with the same brush with which they tarred him, that of lacking integrity and agitating for some sort of political advantage.

---

### Additional Notes §21

---

**5:7** / See V. C. Pfitzner, *Paul and the Agon Motif* (NovTSup 16; Leiden: E. J. Brill, 1967), esp. pp. 136–38.

**5:8** / The Greek word for **persuasion** *(peismonē)* occurs only here in the NT, and outside the NT it occurs rarely. Longenecker notes that later extrabiblical writings use the word with negative connotations to mean "empty rhetoric" *(Galatians,* p. 231). Paul may be using the word with this nuance, thereby denigrating his rivals' message as empty in distinction from his, which is "the truth."

**5:10** / In the Greek the word *krima,* here translated "penalty," is lit. "judgment." The word translated "pay" *(bastasei)* has the sense of "bearing" or "enduring."

**5:11** / Given that Paul states that his coming to faith in Christ was also a call to preach to Gentiles as Gentiles (1:16), it is doubtful that by **still preaching circumcision** Paul means that in his early Christian days he preached circumcision. The Acts account of Paul circumcising Timothy (16:3) is problematic. As mentioned in the Introduction, many scholars now tend to deal with discrepancies between Paul's self-presentation and the account in Acts by giving priority to Paul's own words. Even if the incident in Acts 16 did occur, it is to be noted that since he was the son of a Jewish mother, Timothy was effectively a Jew and not a Gentile.

Donaldson suggests that Paul is speaking of his former life as an advocate for Judaism to the Gentiles; the sense is: "In my former life in Judaism I admit that I preached circumcision to the Gentiles; but then God called me to preach Christ crucified, and I preach circumcision no longer" (*Paul and the Gentiles*, pp. 282–83).

## §22 Paul's Gospel Offers Freedom and Right Living through the Spirit (Gal. 5:13–18)

**5:13** / Completing the wish of the previous verse, Paul declares that rather than listening to the "agitators," the Galatians should recognize their true call. Paul has earlier described the Galatians' Christian life as the result of a call (1:6; 5:8). Now he says they **were called to be free.** Freedom is one of the chief ways Paul has described the life in Christ that he preaches (2:4), and it provides a rich descriptive concept for his understanding of the gospel (4:22–31). To his Galatian readers it should be more than plain by now that, from Paul's perspective, freedom is synonymous with the message he preaches (5:1).

But Paul recognizes that his understanding of freedom may differ from that of others. For him it is clear that the freedom of the gospel is not the freedom of self-indulgence but the freedom to **serve one another.** For those with philosophical or religious sensibilities, then as now, Paul's statement is a truism. Self-indulgence is slavery of a sort, and the capacity and opportunity to love is freedom.

The command to be slaves to each other is, however, a strikingly dramatic way of expressing the nature of the love believers are freed to demonstrate. Paul may refer to slaves as a contrasting metaphor to freedom, but the concept also resonates with his self-understanding (1:10; 2 Cor. 4:5), in which he imitates his Lord, who took the form of a slave (Phil. 2:7). The life of believers is focused on emulating the life of Christ—the one who, as Paul puts it earlier in the letter, "loved me and gave himself" (2:20). In this way, not through circumcision, believers' freedom is correctly embodied.

A discussion of the practical possibilities of the religious disposition for which Paul has been arguing now follows. Most of Paul's letters contain a similar section, often called the "paraenetic" or ethical section of the letter. In this segment of Galatians

Paul turns from his negative attack on the advocates of circumcision to a positive presentation of the life in Christ. This section also responds to any concern the Galatian believers would have about how to know what is ethically right. Since this concern helped make them open to the influence of the rival evangelists, it is important for Paul to articulate the ethical benefits of life in Christ.

The desire for personal and political freedom was as strong in the ancient Mediterranean world as it is now. Philo wrote: "freedom is the noblest of human blessings" (*Good Person* 139 [Colson, LCL]). Plato understands freedom as one of the virtues of the soul along with self-restraint, justice, courage, and truth (*Phaedo* 115a). The philosophers thought much about how one could be free, especially about how one could be free of the internal passions and impulses that enslave each human being. Philosophies promised happiness and freedom through conversion to different approaches to life. Philo wrote: "slavery then is applied in one sense to bodies, in another to souls; bodies have men for their masters, souls their vices and passions. The same is true of freedom; one freedom produces a security of the body from men of superior strength, the other sets the mind at liberty from the domination of the passions" (*Good Person* 17 [Colson, LCL]). Epictetus said:

> I can show you a free man. . . . Diogenes was free. How did that come? It was not because he was born of free parents, for he was not, but because he himself was free, because he had cast off all the handles of slavery, and there was no way in which a person could get close and lay hold of him to enslave him. Everything he had was easily loosed. . . . If you had laid hold of his property, he would have let it go rather than followed you for its sake; if you had laid hold of his leg, he would have let his leg go. (*Arrian's Discourses* 4.1.152–55 [Oldfather, LCL])

In identifying his message with freedom Paul was appealing to an aspiration prevalent in his culture, at least among those of a philosophical nature or blessed with the time to reflect.

From what the extant texts tell us, the ancient world sought freedom within the law rather than freedom as the opposite of law. Judaism thought of law abiding as the road to freedom, as did Jewish Christianity (cf. Jas. 1:25; 2:8–13). This was also true of non-Jewish ancients. Aristotle wrote: "it is preferable for the law to rule than any one of the citizens" (*Pol.* 3.11.2 [Rackham, LCL]); and "the law is wisdom without desire" (*Pol.* 3.11.5;

ibid.). Freedom was to be found in the context of law. Dio Chrysostom defined freedom "as the knowledge of what is allowable [by law and custom] and what is forbidden, and slavery as ignorance of what is allowed and what is not" (*Fourteenth Discourse: Slavery* 1.18 [Cohoon, LCL]).

This general attitude toward law may go some way to explaining why Paul is comfortable speaking of law in the same context as freedom (5:14). The freedom in Christ is not a freedom from orderliness or communal life or concern for others. Rather, Paul's vision of the Christian life is one that includes the highest interpersonal standard, that of serving others. His argument is specifically against the Mosaic law as a necessary requirement for Gentile believers. The freedom Paul extols is not anarchic but anti-Torah.

**5:14** / Paul seeks to co-opt the power that the concept of **law** has with his readers, saying that he can sum up the law **in a single command.** He wishes to assure the Galatians that his gospel incorporates the **entire** law as far as it concerns ethics. But his gospel has incorporated the law in simplified form—a "single command"—for the law is fulfilled not through works but faith. And the faith through which the law is fulfilled works through love (5:6), that is, through being "in Christ." Therefore the law is not an addition to faith but is completed through faith.

It seems paradoxical that after spending so much time arguing for freedom from the law, Paul should be concerned to explain how the law could be fulfilled. Yet, for two reasons it may have been important for Paul to make this statement. First, if it is the case that the Galatians were concerned with how to fulfill the demands of justice in their new law-free religious context, Paul may consider it prudent to frame a response in which he addresses this concern. Second, his statement gains the upper hand over the troublemakers' claim to be the ones to have correctly contextualized belief in Christ. The rival evangelists considered that believers in Christ had to become law-observant Jews. Paul's conviction is that to be a believer in Christ is to be a recipient of the promises given by God to the Jewish people but now extended to all. Having the law written on the heart was one of the promises (Jer. 31:33), and Paul may be claiming that believers in his gospel know the fulfillment of this promise.

The words **summed up** are a translation of the Greek word *peplērōmati,* often rendered "fulfilled" (see Rom. 8:4; 13:8, where it speaks of fulfilling the law). There is no precedent in Jewish texts for using the word "fulfill" or "complete" in relation to the law (so Barclay, *Obeying the Truth*, p. 138). In this statement, then, Paul expresses his unique vision that in Christ God's purposes are realized, even the purposes previously articulated in the law.

Love for others is defined as the same as love for self: **love your neighbor as yourself.** Just as there is no escaping the necessity and wholesomeness of loving oneself, so in the Christian community there is no escaping the necessity and wholesomeness of loving others.

Paul's directive to "serve one another in love" can also be translated "become slaves of one another." The place of the slave was a position to be eschewed in the ancient world. Rare indeed was the philosopher or religious writer who would use the image of slave in a positive light, even metaphorically. Aristotle wrote: "one who is a human being belonging by nature not to himself but to another is by nature a slave" (*Pol.* 1.2.7 [Rackham, LCL]). Paul describes the kind of love that can fulfill the law as producing the kind of life required of a slave—a life lived entirely for others.

**5:15** / Paul then approaches the nature of Christian freedom from the negative point of view, saying that if the Galatians **keep on biting and devouring each other** they will be **destroyed by each other.** This image works on the basis of understanding believers as indentured to other believers (having become slaves to each other) by all being in Christ. The ethical life based on being "in Christ" works because of the organic nature of Christian community: if they bite and devour one another, they too will be destroyed.

**5:16** / Paul directs his readers to **live by the Spirit.** The Greek word translated "live" *(peripateite)* is literally "walk." Paul uses this word elsewhere when speaking of living the new life in Christ (Rom. 6:4), a life that is conducted by means of the Spirit (Rom. 8:4). The word suggests continuance, progress, and daily attention. Paul commands his readers to avoid gratifying **the desires of the sinful nature** by means not of law observance but of living by the Spirit.

The Greek for "sinful nature" is literally "flesh" *(sarx).* As Paul invests this term with all that is against the Spirit, the translation "sinful nature" largely hits the mark. The word "desires" is singular in the Greek, expressing the sense that existence in the flesh is an existence characterized by desire. Philosophical and religious thinkers in the ancient world understood that desire was intrinsic to human nature and that it was a trap from which it was necessary to be freed. Desire means one makes one's happiness or peace hostage to achieving or receiving what one desires, whether it be money, position, or another person. Epictetus said: "For freedom is not acquired by satisfying yourself with what you desire, but by destroying your desire" (*Arrian's Discourses* 4.1.175 [Oldfather, LCL]). Xenophon has Socrates say:

> Some are ruled by gluttony, some by fornication, some by drunkenness, and some by foolish and expensive ambitions which rule cruelly over any men they get into their power, as long as they see that they are in their prime and able to work; so cruelly indeed, that they force them to bring whatever they have earned by working and to spend it on their desires. But when they perceive that they are unable to work because of age, they abandon them to a wreched old age and they try to use others as their slaves." (*Economics* 1.23; trans. Pomeroy, p. 111)

The Jewish thinker Philo advocated circumcision for "the excision of pleasure and all passions" (*On the Migration of Abraham* 92 [Colson and Whitaker, LCL]). A Christian thinker subsequent to Paul expresses a similar understanding of the goal of the Christian life: "One must live without city or home; one must have nothing of one's own—no friends, no possessions, no livelihood, no business, no company; one must renounce human learning and prepare the heart to receive the impressions of divine instructions" (Basil, *Letter 2;* quoted from Wiles and Santer, *Documents in Early Christian Thought*, p. 212).

In distinction from Greco-Roman philosophical and Jewish approaches to the problem of desire, Paul understands that freedom from enslavement to desire comes through living by the Spirit. Life "in Christ" involves the will of the believer: a conscious and continual turning away from that which is opposed to the Spirit. Even after faith in Christ believers must combat the desire to be self-serving, to live for their own comfort rather than to open themselves to the expansive love required of and available to those in Christ.

**5:17** / Paul portrays the human dilemma as one in which even the best of intentions are thwarted by the limitations of human nature. Paul's description of the problem is that people **do not do what** they **want.** Unlike philosophical and religious systems that advocate a rule of life that might gradually free people from enslavement to desire, Paul advocates human will (v. 16) in cooperation with the transforming work of the Spirit.

Paul's advice is an acknowlegment that there are daily struggles for those "in Christ"; that ethical dilemmas and failures remain part of believers' lives. Paul does not promise immediate transformation or sanctification, but he does offer hope that while **the sinful nature desires what is contrary to the Spirit,** so **the Spirit what is contrary to the sinful nature.**

**5:18** / Earlier in the letter Paul affirmed the Galatians' experience of the Spirit (3:2–5), which, along with his connecting of the promise to Abraham with the promise of the Spirit (3:14), suggests that the Galatians' self-understanding was as those who were **led by the Spirit.** The sentence structure in verse 18 also suggests that the Galatians regarded themselves as those who knew the Spirit. The consequence of this fact is that they are then **not under law.** The subtext is Paul's assertion that they do not need to accept the rival evangelists' offer of law in order to live well. The plain sense is that there are two contrasting and mutually exclusive ways of approaching the ethical choices in life: through the guidance of the Spirit or through the guidance of the law.

---

### Additional Notes §22

---

**5:13** / In the Greek the term translated **sinful nature** is "flesh" *(sarx).* "Flesh" is not always a term laden with negative theological connotations. It can mean "body" (e.g., 4:13, where Paul speaks of his "illness" [NIV] or "weakness of the flesh"). The Christian life is lived "in the body/flesh" (2:20). Yet the term is also used to indicate that which is opposed to the Spirit (["human effort"] 3:3; ["ordinary way"] 4:29). The latter sense is the one Paul intends in this verse, making the NIV's translation "sinful nature" appropriate.

For a good overview of the position of slaves in the ancient Mediterranean world, see D. Martin, *Slavery as Salvation: The Metaphor of Slavery in Pauline Christianity* (New Haven: Yale University Press, 1990), pp. 1–49.

**5:14** / The statement that **the entire law is summed up in a single command: "Love your neighbor as yourself"** is not unique to Paul. This command from Lev. 19:18 is found both on the lips of Jesus (Matt. 22:40) and Rabbi Akiba: "R. Aqiba said, 'You shall love your

neighbor as yourself . . . is the encompassing principle of the Torah' "
(*Genesis Rabbah 24.7 on Genesis 5:1,* quoted from J. Neusner, *Genesis
Rabbah,* vol. 1 [Atlanta: Scholars, 1985], p. 270). Paul shared this under-
standing and cites it here and in Rom. 13:9.

**5:18** / Paul used the phrase "under law" previously as a way
to describe life without Christ (3:23; 4:5). Elsewhere he equates being
led by the Spirit with being children of God (Rom. 8:14).

## §23 Vices from Which the Spirit Can Provide Freedom (Gal. 5:19–21)

**5:19** / So as to concretize the contrast between the flesh **(sinful nature)** and the Spirit, Paul says that the flesh results in certain **acts.** The phrase "acts of sinful nature" has a counterpart in 5:22—"fruit of the Spirit." Vice and virtue lists such as the one Paul provides in 5:19–26 were a common feature of philosophical and religious writings in ancient times, and Paul has chosen to list **obvious** actions that indicate what he calls a sinful nature—actions that result in damage to self and to relationships. As Sanders notes, "proper behaviour is self-evident" (*Paul and Palestinian Judaism,* p. 513). Several of the actions Paul lists are ones that Jews typically characterized as Gentile vices (see these listed in 1 Pet. 4:3). Perhaps in response to the "agitators' " presentation of the need for law so as to avoid such Gentile vices, Paul declares that the remedy is life in the Spirit.

The first three actions concern sexuality. **Sexual immorality** refers to illicit sexual relations. This was an issue in Paul's churches, for on several occasions he warns against this (1 Thess. 4:3; 1 Cor. 6:18). **Impurity** appears also to refer to sexual immorality, perhaps in reference to violence in connection with sexual activity. Paul connects it with "sexual immorality" and "debauchery" in 2 Corinthians 12:21. **Debauchery** means "wantonness" or "licentiousness." In this context it suggests sexual licentiousness or abandon.

**5:20** / Although Paul wants to separate his converts from law keeping, he maintains the characteristic Jewish antipathy toward **idolatry** (cf. 1 Cor. 10:14). Paul knows there to be one God (Gal. 3:20) who cannot be worshiped in idols. **Witchcraft** has the sense of "magic" and the use of drugs for magical purposes, which might be called black magic. This practice was regarded as offensive and dangerous by Jews (see Isa. 47:9; also Exod. 7:11, 22) and others in the Greco-Roman world. Plato writes about the dangers of "sorcery and magic" and prescribes punishments for wizards who injure others by means of sorcery (*Laws* 11.933). Plato warns also against "that class of monstrous natures who . . . in contempt of mankind conjure the souls of the living and say that they can conjure the dead and promise to charm the Gods with sacrifices and prayer" (*Laws* 909b; trans. Jowett). Under the Roman emperors sorcery became a punishable offense. **Hatred** indicates "hostile feelings and actions" (so BAGD, p. 331). The vices listed in the rest of the verse identify manifestations of hatred. **Discord** has also the meaning of strife or contention; **jealousy** or envy (cf. Rom. 13:13) suggests, as Burton puts so well, "the eager desire for possession created by the spectacle of another's possession" (*Galatians*, p. 307); the word for **fits of rage** connotes intense anger. **Selfish ambition** is a difficult word to translate but bears the sense of self-seeking, strife, and contentiousness. **Dissensions** refer to divisiveness in a group (cf. Rom. 16:17); and **factions** (cf. 1 Cor. 11:19) to groups who hold to their opinions aggressively and divisively.

**5:21** / The list continues by identifying **envy,** which is similar to "jealousy" and carries the sense of malice. **Drunkenness** can also be read as "drinking bouts" (cf. Rom. 13:13). In connection with **orgies** the word suggests the drunken abandon that was a feature of ancient life at certain festivals.

Paul ends with a warning, **as I did before.** His current warning is consonant with what he said previously and would undercut any criticism from the rival evangelists that Paul's law-free gospel was a license for vice or that he had not adequately taught his converts about ethical behavior. Paul states emphatically his conviction that **those who live like this will not inherit the kingdom of God.** Paul's choice of the word "inherit" resonates with the theme of inheritance, the understanding of which has been a battleground between himself and his opponents. Until this point Paul has stressed that his converts can be assured of inheriting the promise to Abraham by virtue of being in Christ. Now he reshapes the theme somewhat. Inheritance can be lost through acting in accordance with the flesh (the "sinful nature"), which is another way of saying that it is necessary to remain "in Christ" to share in the inheritance. The flesh is that which is opposed to the Spirit (5:17), and the Spirit is the promise to Abraham realized among Gentile believers in Christ (3:14). To live in accordance with the "sinful nature" is to exclude oneself from the inheritance.

## Additional Notes §23

**5:19** / The Greek word translated "acts" is lit. "works" *(erga)*, a word that Paul used in the phrase "works of law" (2:16) and contrasted to the Spirit (3:2) and faith (3:5). The word has a negative connotation for him. This is the only occurrence of the phrase "works of flesh" **(acts of the sinful nature)** in Paul's writings. We should not be too quick to understand it as equivalent to "works of law," particularly since the works listed are largely prohibited by the law. Paul's later understanding that the law provided an opportunity for sin (Rom. 7:7–25) is not in view here.

**5:21** / The word **live** is a rendering of a Greek present participle *(prassontes)* that means "those who are given to practice." The warning is directed at those who consciously and repeatedly indulge in these vices.

Unlike the gospel writers, Paul does not often use the phrase **the kingdom of God.** On occasion he uses it in ethical contexts (1 Cor. 6:9–10; Rom. 14:17) but also in other settings (1 Cor. 4:20; 15:24, 50; 1 Thess. 2:12). This is the only use of the phrase in Galatians. Perhaps Paul is reminding his readers of his original preaching or responding to the "confusers" by using a term they had introduced into the Galatian churches.

## §24 The Fruit of the Spirit (Gal. 5:22–26)

**5:22** / Paul now turns to the **fruit of the Spirit.** The designation of the manifestations of the Spirit as "fruit" speaks volumes about Paul's understanding of the ways of life he has been contrasting throughout the letter. Life lived in the flesh ("sinful nature") is a life of work ("acts"), a life that strives and strains for the protection of self and often consequently for the domination of others. Life in the Spirit, on the other hand, blossoms, and the word "fruit" gives the sense that the characteristics Paul lists in verses 22 and 23 are the result of a healthy rooted state such as comes from living in Christ. Note that "fruit" is in the singular, and so the following qualities are various aspects of the generative power of the Spirit. Most of these aspects of the fruit of the Spirit are characteristics Paul elsewhere attributes to God. For Paul the fruit of the Spirit generates godly characteristics in the believer.

The first characteristic is **love,** which Paul has identified with Christ (2:20) and with the life of those in Christ (5:6, 14). The next is **joy,** which is not the same as happiness. Joy is not a state in which most of the circumstances of one's life are satisfactory, but rather is life rooted in the Spirit (Rom. 14:17) and in God (Rom. 15:13). **Peace,** like joy, stems not from the external circumstances of one's life but from the God of peace (Rom. 15:33; 16:20; Phil. 4:9). **Patience** has the sense of forbearance and is a characteristic of God (Rom. 2:4; 9:22) in which believers share (cf. 2 Cor. 6:6). **Kindness** is another feature of God's character (Rom. 2:4; 11:22) that should characterize the people of God (2 Cor. 6:6). **Goodness** has the sense of "generosity" or "uprightness." Paul uses it as a high compliment (Rom. 15:14) and recognizes that only through God's power can believers exhibit such a virtue (2 Thess. 1:11). **Faithfulness** is another feature of God's character (1 Cor. 1:9; 10:13; 2 Cor. 1:18; 1 Thess. 5:24; 2 Thess. 3:3). It is also one of the chief characteristics of Christ (2:16; 3:22).

**5:23** / **Gentleness** has the meaning of "humility," "courtesy," or "considerateness." It is the most appropriate and constructive attitude to have in relating to others (cf. Gal. 6:1). Paul speaks of Christ as having this quality (2 Cor. 10:1). **Self-control**—the mastery of one's own desires, or, as Plato puts it "a man being his own master" (*Republic* 430e; trans. Jowett; cf. *Republic* 390b)—was a major ethical goal in the philosophies of the ancient Mediterranean world. Xenophon defends Socrates as a man of self-control in word and deed and extols self-control as "the foundation of all virtue" (*Memorabilia* 1.5.4 [Marchant, LCL]). Paul also recognizes it as a worthy goal (cf. 1 Cor. 7:9; 9:25).

The fruit of the Spirit cannot be produced or prohibited by **law.** Life in Christ will result in character that fulfills the law apart from the law (cf. 5:14).

**5:24–26** / This is so because **those who belong to Christ Jesus have crucified the sinful nature** with **its passions and desires.** Such belonging is the means by which believers can live righteously. Earlier Paul said that he understood himself to "have been crucified with Christ" so that it was no longer he who lived but Christ who lived in him (2:19–20). This sharing in Christ's death results in justification (2:21). Justification results in a new status in God's sight and a new way of behaving. Through belonging to Christ (cf. 3:29) believers participate in the death of Christ and so, as Paul puts it in Romans, "we know that our old self was crucified with him so that the body of sin might be rendered powerless, that we might no longer be slaves to sin" (Rom. 6:6).

Paul now ties together what he has been saying: **since we live by the Spirit, let us keep in step with the Spirit.** Paul has directed believers to "live by the Spirit" (cf. 5:16) and claimed that they are "led by the Spirit" (5:18). Now he shifts the emphasis by stating that the basis of their life is that they are those who "live by the Spirit." On this basis he calls them to be guided by the Spirit. By means of the Spirit the Galatian believers are to enact the life they already have in the Spirit. The NEB translates it this way: "If the Spirit is the source of our life, let the Spirit also direct our course."

Finally, Paul warns his readers not to **become conceited, provoking and envying each other.** At first this exhortation appears to belong more properly with 5:19–21. It may be, however, that Paul emphasizes these vices after his exhortation to keep in step with the Spirit because they are the most detrimental to a Spirit-led life. Conceit can be detrimental to participation in the Spirit (cf. Paul's warning against conceit, Phil. 2:3). Provocation is contrary to an essential feature of life in the Spirit—unity (cf. 1 Cor. 12:4–13). Envy can also be the basis of disruptive, aggressive, and destructive behavior. These three traits may be particular problems for people who are contending for recognition of their spiritual gifts and for the upper hand in spirituality (cf. 1 Cor. 12–14). Paul includes himself in his exhortation to keep in step with the Spirit and in the following exhortation (v. 26).

---

### Additional Notes §24

---

**5:23** / The statement **against such things there is no law** has a parallel in Aristotle. In *Politics* he writes of those who are exceptionally virtuous that "against such people there is no law" (3.13.2 [1284a]; my translation). Longenecker suggests that this sentiment may have had a proverbial status in the ancient world to express "actions that surpass all legal prescriptions and are therefore beyond any legal accounting" (*Galatians*, p. 264).

**5:24** / Dying to **passions** was a goal of the ancient philosophies. We find it also in writings of Philo. For instance, Philo commends "the light of Isaac—the generic form of happiness, of the joy and gladness which belongs to those who have ceased from the manner of women [Gen. xviii.11] and died to the passions" (*On the Cherubim* 8 [Colson and Whitaker, LCL]). See also Philo, *On Husbandry* 17. Plato writes:

> This then is why a man should be of good cheer about his soul, who in his life has rejected the pleasures and ornaments of the body, thinking they are alien to him and more likely to do him harm than good, and ... after adorning his soul with no alien ornaments, but with its own proper adornment of self-restraint and justice and courage and freedom and truth, awaits his departure to the other world, ready to go when fate calls him. (*Phaedo* 114–115a [Fowler, LCL])

The goal Paul presents is not peculiar to him, although the means—dying with Christ—is uniquely Christian.

**5:25** / Unlike the word translated "live" in v. 16 (lit. "walk"), the Greek word *zōmen* translated **live** in this verse lit. is "live." The nuance is somewhat different in each case: in v. 16 the word gives the sense of continual active participation in the Spirit; in v. 25 it indicates the basis of one's life.

The phrase **keep in step with the Spirit** contains the verbal form of the word "elements" *(stoichōmen)* encountered in 4:3 and 4:9. In its verbal form it has the sense of walking in a straight line and so of conducting oneself appropriately. The same verb occurs in Gal. 6:16, being translated as "follow." Here it means walking, by means of the Spirit, in the path set by the Spirit.

# §25 Life Together in the Spirit (Gal. 6:1–10)

**6:1** / Addressing his readers as **brothers**, Paul turns to a fuller description of how a community living by the Spirit should behave. He first says that **if someone is caught in a sin** those **who are spiritual should restore him gently.** In contrast to 5:21, where Paul warned that those who do sinful acts would not inherit the kingdom of God, here Paul addresses the practical situation of a believer doing wrong. This circumstance does not call for the believer to be excommunicated or handed over to Satan (cf. 1 Cor. 5:5). Instead, the transgressor is to be restored, "put in order," corrected for his or her own good. Paul spends greater time on the manner and special dangers of the ones who might be called on to restore the transgressor than he does on the transgressor. In this regard Betz comments that "Paul seems keenly aware that a self-righteous posture of prosecutors can cause greater damage to the community than the offense done by a wrongdoer" (*Galatians*, p. 298). The "spiritual" ones are to do their work "gently," that is, they are to demonstrate the fruit of the Spirit (5:23) even while they correct. Their role will put them in spiritual danger, and so Paul warns them not to be **tempted.** They can avoid temptation by being watchful. The correctors should spend as much time keeping an eye on themselves as they do on the offender.

**6:2** / The practical issue of transgression in the Christian community leads Paul to give the umbrella instruction to **carry each other's burdens** (see also 5:13–14). This disposition allows fulfillment of **the law of Christ.** The way of Christ, as demonstrated in his life and death ("he loved and gave himself" Gal. 2:20), is to bear the burdens of others. Even the transgressor's burdens are to be borne (cf. Rom. 15:1).

It may be that the troublemakers had been using the phrase "law of Christ" when arguing that faith included the requirement of circumcision, in which case Paul appropriates this term in order to turn it against his opponents. The "law of Christ" does not require Torah observance, but instead it allows one to act as Christ, the one who endured even death on a cross for the sake of others (cf. Phil. 2:4–11).

If the phrase "law of Christ" is not one that Paul took over from his opponents, the rhetorical effect of bringing together two terms that until this point have been mutually exclusive— law and Christ—would have been dramatic, thereby redefining the meaning of law in light of Christ. Law now is that which is fulfilled through love.

**6:3–10** / Even as believers bear each other's burdens **each one should carry his own load.** The way of Christ and of living in Christ is not for believers to shirk responsibility for their own character; it requires self-examination. Paul directs his readers to **test** their **own actions.** This extends the thought of 6:1, in which Paul warns recognized spiritual individuals to keep an eye on themselves even in the course of dealing with the transgression of another. The focus of believers' lives is both outward and inward; outward toward others, while attending to the development of their own character through careful and honest assessment of their activity. This will ensure that in and of itself the life of each believer is a cause of **pride,** a source of gratification.

The statement **if anyone thinks he is something when he is nothing, he deceives himself** may be a truism Paul uses as a warning. If those who clearly have nothing to boast about are self-deceived enough to boast, then there is real danger that those who have so much (i.e., the Galatians) can be even more deceived.

In a statement as sweeping as that of 6:2a Paul writes **a man reaps what he sows.** Paul qualifies it with the stern observation that **God cannot be mocked.** In other words, God cannot be treated with contempt. Human beings' actions determine outcomes. God sees all, as the **harvest** will demonstrate (cf. 2 Cor. 5:10). If people **sow** to **please** their **sinful nature** the outcome will be **destruction.** If, however, they sow **to please the Spirit,** they will **reap eternal life.** Paul closes by advocating that the key is that **as we have opportunity, let us do good to all people, especially to those who belong to the family of believers.** The Greek word translated here as opportunity *(kairon)* is the same word as was translated "time" in the previous verse. The sense is "while we have time," thereby alluding to the fact that believers live in expectation of the end. The phrase "family of believers" is literally "household of faith." The designation "faith" for belief in Christ occurs throughout Galatians (e.g., 1:23). Now Paul describes those who share such faith as a family. This final injunction stresses the importance of attending particularly to the needs of believers and directs the attention of believers to all human beings (cf. 1 Tim. 2:1–5).

---

### Additional Notes §25

---

**6:1** / The **spiritual** ones is a term also used in 1 Cor. (e.g., 1 Cor. 2:13, 15; 12:1; 14:37), where Paul directs his attention to the concerns of a Spirit-filled community.

The term **restore** *(katartizete)* is used in Hellenistic philosophical literature for the task of the philosopher who is called to restore himself and others to, as Plutarch records Cato saying, "conformity with his best interests" *(Cato the Younger* 65.5 [Perrin, LCL]).

**6:2** / While this is Paul's only use of the phrase **law of Christ** he does use a similar phrase in 1 Cor. 9:21 (see also Rom. 8:2). Some scholars have interpreted the phrase to mean that Paul thought that Jesus, the Jewish Messiah, brought in the anticipated messianic Torah, which consisted primarily of the ethical teaching of Jesus, "the law of Christ" (so Davies, *Paul and Rabbinic Judaism,* pp. 69–74, 142–45, 174–76; and P. Stuhlmacher, "The Law as a Topic of Biblical Theology," in *Reconciliation, Law, Righteousness: Essays in Biblical Theology* [Philadelphia: Fortress, 1986], pp. 110–33). Others, noting the connection between this verse and 5:14, suggest that it means the Mosaic law as "redefined and fulfilled by Christ in love" (Barclay, *Obeying the Truth,* p. 134). Martyn understands the phrase to refer "to the Law as it has been taken in hand by Christ himself" *(Galatians,* p. 549). Others leave aside the Mosaic law and understand the phrase as a reference to the law of love. C. K. Barrett writes that the "law of Christ" is "virtually indistinguishable from the law of love in 5:14" *(Freedom and Obligation: A Study of the Epistle to the Galatians* [London: SPCK, 1985], p. 83).

**6:6** / The direction that **anyone who receives instruction in the word must share all good things with his instructor** was a common understanding particularly in Pythagoreanism, Epicureanism, and Stoicism. It could refer to sharing both material goods and the virtuous goods gained from living the philosophical life. Paul's general position was that sharing financial resources was a good thing (see 1 Cor. 9:11; cf. Rom. 15:27) and that teachers should be able to receive financial support (1 Cor. 9:3–14). Paul was willing to receive financial assistance from those he trusted (Phil. 4:15–16).

**6:8** / While the promise of **eternal life** has not been central to this letter (cf. Rom. 2:7; 5:21; 6:22–23), at the opening of the letter Paul declared that Christ had set believers free from the "present evil age," which implies understanding this age as the finite age of time and assumes there will be an eternal age.

**6:9** / The phrase **at the proper time** bears the sense of "at the appropriate moment." It may have an eschatological meaning: at the end time all people will reap according to what they have sown (cf. 1 Cor. 4:5).

## §26 Closing (Gal. 6:11–18)

The closing of Pauline letters have several standard features, among them a blessing of grace (e.g., 1 Cor. 16:23; 2 Cor. 13:14; Phil. 4:23), a wish for peace (e.g., Rom. 15:33; 2 Cor. 13:11b; Phil. 4:9b; 1 Thess. 5:23), and greetings (e.g., Rom. 16:3–16; 1 Cor. 16:20b; 2 Cor. 13:12a; Phil. 4:21a; 1 Thess. 5:23). In Galatians the blessing of grace appears at 16:18 and the wish for peace at 6:16. There is, however, a conspicuous absence of any greetings. This is particularly noteworthy because Paul had a personal history with the Galatians (4:12–15). This absence, like that of any thanksgiving at the letter opening, probably signals that Paul is so focused on persuading and warning the Galatians that he either does not take the time for niceties or deliberately omits a thanksgiving and greetings so as to underscore the seriousness of his tone.

**6:11** / Paul brings his letter to a close, switching from dictation to writing for himself—**see what large letters I use as I write to you with my own hand!** Paul, like many other ancient writers, used a secretary or trained copyist (the letter to the Romans names the scribe—"I, Tertius, who wrote down this letter" [16:22]). Sometimes at the end of his letters Paul would write a few lines in his own hand (see 1 Cor. 16:21). One reason for this practice was that it discouraged forgery (see 2 Thess. 3:17).

**6:12–15** / Paul does not close his letter with an easy denouement but again warns his readers of the influence of the rival evangelists. He characterizes them as **those who want to make a good impression outwardly** and **are trying to compel the Galatians to be circumcised.** The Greek contains the word "flesh," and so reads literally "good showing in the flesh." As Paul has used the word "flesh" throughout the letter for that which is opposed to the Spirit (e.g., 5:17), he may be denigrating the rival evangelists by caricaturing them as concerned about the flesh, not the things of God. His statement is also a question:

Would you want such as these to be the ones to compel you to be circumcised?

Paul returns to the central issue: **the cross of Christ.** This he has referred to earlier as an "offense" (5:11) that could be removed by circumcision. The integrity of preaching Christ crucified to Gentiles involves discounting circumcision. Paul believes that faith in Christ involves co-crucifixion with Christ (2:19; 5:24). This all-encompassing and undoubtedly difficult involvement "in Christ" is adequate for justification and salvation.

Paul knew that to preach the cross of Christ the way he did was to be **persecuted** (5:11). To avoid such persecution is to disavow the cross of Christ.

Paul seeks further to discredit his opponents' position by asserting that **even those who are circumcised** do not **obey the law.** The Greek "those who are circumcised" *(hoi peritemnomenoi)* is a present middle/passive participle. It can be translated either "those who are circumcising" or "those who receive circumcision." That is, it can refer either to Paul's opponents or to his converts. There is no evidence thus far in the letter that some among Paul's Galatian Gentile readers had already received circumcision. Rather, the situation appears to be that though some are close to receiving circumcision (5:3), Paul feels he has a window of opportunity in which to dissuade them. For this reason and because Paul refers to his opponents in the rest of the verse **(they want you to be circumcised)**, it is best to understand the participle as referring to the rival evangelists. By saying that even his circumcised opponents do not obey **the law** Paul may be not so much calling their law observance into question as repeating his thesis: if they did obey the law they would see that the law upholds his position (cf. 4:21–5:1).

Paul now contrasts himself with the circumcisers. Their agenda is to **boast about** the Galatian believers' **flesh.** His way is to **boast** of nothing **except . . . the cross of our Lord Jesus Christ.** Paul implicitly casts the agitators among those who do not belong to Jesus Christ. By advocating circumcision for Gentiles they demonstrate that they are not "those who belong to Christ Jesus [and] have crucified the sinful nature (flesh)" (5:24).

In 6:12 Paul charged that the rival evangelists were concerned only with their flesh. Here he charges that his opponents want to circumcise so that they may boast about his readers' flesh. This statement conveys the sense that the consequence of circumcision would allow for boasting only of flesh and not of Spirit. Circumcision would plant his readers in the realm of flesh.

Paul repeats his earlier assertion that **neither circumcision nor uncircumision means anything** (cf. 5:6). **What counts is a new creation.** This new creation is obviously something different from the current **world.** It signifies newness in everything—a beginning again that occurs "in Christ" (cf. 2 Cor. 5:18–19). The concern with circumcision looks to the past, clinging to categories and practices that have no place in the new creation and hinder one from participating in it.

**6:16** / Paul blesses **all who follow this rule** with **peace and mercy.** At the beginning of his letter Paul cursed the one preaching a gospel other than his (1:8–9), and here he blesses those who adhere to his standard and calls them the **Israel of God.** The flip side of this blessing is a curse on those who do not follow this rule; although they may claim to be Israel, they are not truly so.

This is the only time that the phrase **Israel of God** appears in Paul's letters. Elsewhere he refers to Jews as "Israel according to the flesh" (1 Cor. 10:18). In Galatians at least, he did not think of Israel according to the flesh as the true Israel (cf. Rom. 2:17–29; 9–11). While he does not elsewhere claim the name Israel for believers in Christ, he does so here. This phrase is similar to the "church of God" (Gal. 1:13). It may have been used by the circumcisers to assert that they were the true Israel of God, in which case Paul is here coopting the term; or it may have been Paul's own invention. In either case it indicates that Paul is battling with his opponents over who can correctly understand the role of the law for believers in Christ.

**6:17** / Paul appeals that no one should **cause** him **trouble.** He conveys an air of confidence that his letter will accomplish its task and that in the future he will no longer be troubled by this situation. Paul knows himself to be one who bears **the marks of Jesus** on his **body.** He is certain of his own integrity and that his position will win the day. And, in terms of the outcome of the struggle between the rival evangelists and himself, he was right.

**6:18** / Paul ends with a grace benediction and an **Amen.** The final word closes the letter on a strong note. Given its character as a word of response, it is also Paul's final invitation for his readers fully to accept his message.

## Additional Notes §26

**6:12** / It is not unknown for Paul to end his letters with a warning (see Rom. 16:17–20), although more typically he ends with an exhortation (e.g., 1 Cor. 16:16; 2 Cor. 13:11).

The word **compel** *(anankazousin)* was used also at 2:14, where it was translated as "force" in the context of reference to forcing Gentiles to live like Jews.

**6:14** / **World** almost always means a sphere in need of redemption because it is in opposition to God (see Rom. 11:15). In 1 Cor., for instance, Paul juxtaposes the spirit of the world with the Spirit of God (2:12).

**6:15** / Paul does not often use the term **new creation,** but the concept is prevalent throughout his writings. The idea that believers have been given a new life (Gal. 2:19–20; cf. Rom. 6:4–6, 11) is key to Paul's understanding of the significance of faith in Christ. Believers know a new life in this present time and also wait for it to be manifested more fully (Rom. 8:18–25).

**6:16** / The phrase **follow this rule** has in the Greek the verb *(stoichēsousin),* found also in 5:25, where it was translated "keep in step." The word "rule" means a "straight edge" or "ruler." It might also be translated "standard."

**6:17** / The Greek for the phrase **marks of Jesus** is *"stigmata* of Jesus." It is impossible to know exactly what these were. They may have been the physical signs of Paul's suffering on behalf of Jesus (see 2 Cor. 6:4–6; 11:23–30). Paul considered that he carried in his very body "the death of Jesus" (2 Cor. 4:10).

# For Further Reading

Barclay, J. M. G. *Obeying the Truth: A Study of Paul's Ethics in Galatians*. Edinburgh: T & T Clark, 1988.

Beker, J. C. *Paul the Apostle: The Triumph of God in Life and Thought*. Philadelphia: Fortress, 1980.

Betz, H. D. *Galatians*. Hermeneia. Philadelphia: Fortress, 1979.

Bruce, F. F. *The Epistle to the Galatians*. The New International Greek Testament Commentary. Grand Rapids: Eerdmans, 1982.

Dahl, N. *The Crucified Messiah and Other Essays*. Minneapolis: Augsburg, 1974.

Davies, W. D. *Paul and Rabbinic Judaism: Some Rabbinic Elements in Pauline Theology*. 4th ed. Philadelphia: Fortress, 1980.

Donaldson, T. L. *Paul and the Gentiles: Remapping the Apostle's Convictional World*. Minneapolis: Fortress, 1997.

Dunn, J. D. G. *A Commentary on the Epistle to the Galatians*. Black's New Testament Commentary. London: A & C Black, 1993. Repr., Peabody, Mass.: Hendrickson, 1993.

_____. *Jesus, Paul and the Law: Studies in Mark and Galatians*. Louisville, Ky.: Westminster John Knox, 1990.

Gaston, L. *Paul and the Torah*. Vancouver: University of British Columbia Press, 1987.

Hays, R. B. *The Faith of Jesus Christ: An Investigation of the Narrative Substructure of Galatians 3:1–4:11*. Chico, Calif.: Scholars, 1983.

Hengel, M., and A. M. Schwemer. *Paul between Damascus and Antioch: The Unknown Years*. Trans. J. Bowden. Louisville, Ky.: Westminster John Knox, 1997.

Hill, C. C. *Hellenists and Hebrews: Reappraising Division within the Earliest Church*. Minneapolis: Fortress, 1992.

Hooker, M. D. *Not Ashamed of the Gospel: New Testament Interpretations of the Death of Christ*. Carlisle: Paternoster, 1994.

Jeremias, J. *Jerusalem in the Time of Jesus*. Trans. F. H. Cave and C. H. Cave. London: SCM, 1969.

Jervis, L. A. "Becoming Like God through Christ: Romans." Pages 143–62 in *Patterns of Discipleship in the New Testament.* Ed. R. N. Longenecker. Grand Rapids: Eerdmans, 1996.

Knox, J. *Chapters in a Life of Paul.* New York: Abingdon, 1950.

Lincoln, A. T. *Paradise Now and Not Yet: Studies in the Role of the Heavenly Dimension in Paul's Thought with Special Reference to His Eschatology.* Cambridge: Cambridge University Press, 1981.

Longenecker, R. N. *Galatians.* WBC 41. Dallas: Word, 1990.

Martyn, J. L. *Galatians.* AB 33A. Garden City, N.Y.: Doubleday, 1997.

Matera, F. J. *Galatians.* Collegeville, Minn.: Liturgical Press, 1992.

Meeks, W. M., and R. L. Wilken, trans. *Jews and Christians in Antioch in the First Four Centuries of the Common Era.* SBLSBS 13. Missoula, Mont.: Scholars, 1978.

Mitchell, S. *Anatolia: Land, Men, and Gods in Asia Minor.* Vol. 1: *The Celts in Anatolia and the Impact of Roman Rule.* Oxford: Clarendon, 1993.

Murphy-O'Connor, J. *Paul: A Critical Life.* Oxford: Clarendon, 1996.

Sanders, E. P. *Paul, the Law and the Jewish People.* Philadelphia: Fortress, 1983.

_____. *Paul and Palestinian Judaism.* Philadelphia: Fortress, 1977.

Segal, A. *Paul the Convert: The Apostolate and Apostasy of Saul the Pharisee.* New Haven: Yale University Press, 1990.

Wallis, I. G. *The Faith of Jesus Christ in Early Christian Traditions.* SNTSMS 84. Ed. M. E. Thrall. Cambridge: Cambridge University Press, 1995.

White, J. L. *Light from Ancient Letters.* Philadelphia: Fortress, 1986.

Wiles, M., and M. Santer, eds. *Documents in Early Christian Thought.* Cambridge: Cambridge University Press, 1975.

Williams, S. K. *Galatians.* Abingdon New Testament Commentaries. Nashville: Abingdon, 1997.

# Subject Index

Herbert, A. G., 21
Hill, C. C., 25, 27, 60
Holmberg, B., 60
Hooker, M. D., 22, 30, 87, 91, 96
Horbury, W., 128
Hulgren, A. J., 29
Hypocrisy, 61

Illness, Paul's, 117–18, 144
"In Christ/Jesus": participation, 23,
132, 135; churches, 48; circumcision,
57; Christ's death, 74; conformity,
75, 119; promise, 94, 108; response
of faith, 102, 105–7, 131; Gentiles
and Jews, 63; 68, 76–77; ethics, 140,
142, 144; adequacy for justification,
158; a new beginning, 159
Inheritance, 4, 32, 86, 92, 95, 102, 105,
108–11, 115, 122, 124, 126, 147
Isaac, 123, 125–26, 128, 151
Ishmael, 123, 125–26, 128
Israel, 4, 7, 16–19, 28, 82–84, 95–96,
99, 103, 110–11, 124, 159
Izates, circumcision of, 65

James: Epistle to, 6, 25, 95; the
apostle, 35, 47, 49, 56, 58–59; the
Lord's brother, 49, 59; the son of
Zebedee, 49; the son of Alphaeus,
49; the son of Mary, 49; the father
of Judas, 49; authority given, 58;
leader of the faith, 59; men from,
52, 61–64, 117
Jeremias, J., 60
Jerusalem (that is above), 123–25, 128
Jervis, L. A., 30, 72
Jewett, R., 120
Jews: loyal to one another, 2; ready
to show compassion, 2; hate and
enmity towards others, 2; revered
by ancients, 3; Christian, 7
John: the disciple, 58–59, 62; the Bap-
tist, 106
Josiah, 124
Joy, 118
Judaism, traditions of, 43–44
Judgment, translated "penalty," 137
Juel, D., 103
Justification: through/by/in faith, 1,
5, 12, 20–22, 54, 68–69, 71–73,
75–76, 85–87, 97, 102, 131; and ob-
serving the law, 20–21, 54, 68–72, 90,

130, 136; and righteousness, 133;
and Christ's death, 150, 158

Kingdom of God, 69, 147–48, 153
Knox, J., 12, 16, 25–28, 45
Kuhn, K. G., 71

Laertius, D., 111
Law, the: as protection, 2; as moral
guidance, 2; observance of, 6, 57,
72, 79–80, 82, 84–86, 90, 95, 103,
111, 115, 117, 129–33, 158; of Moses,
10, 101, 141, 155; of Judaism, 16;
abolished, 17; adoption of, 18, 39;
following, 43, 45, 54, 146; freedom
from, 61, 66; producing virtue, 69;
works of, 69–70, 148; the gospel
adding to, 73; being dead to, 73;
role of, 76, 97, 100–102; fulfilling,
89, 90, 141–42, 150, 154–55; under,
17, 91, 109–10, 112, 122, 127, 144–45;
the end of, 92; relationship to covenant of, 94, 96; giving of, 98; origin
of, 99, 104; ethnic boundary of, 107;
curse of, 5, 91, 126; as wisdom, 140;
written on the heart, 141; proverbial status, 151; of Christ, 153–54
Letters in ancient times: self-identification, 31; addressees, 31, 121;
wish for good health, 31; grace and
peace, 31; Paul identifies co-senders, 32; address, 32; closing, 157
Life: salvific activity, 100; in Christ,
140; eternal, 154, 156
Lightfoot, J. B., 25
Lincoln, A. T., 127
Longenecker, B. W., 24
Longenecker, R. N., 25, 29, 41, 45, 96,
128, 132, 137, 151
Lord, the: origination in Jewish Christian community, 33; appearance
of, 35; Abraham pleases, 84, 94;
day of, 121; confidence in, 135;
Jesus Christ is, 136; assembly of,
137; Paul imitates, 139
Love: law fulfilled in, 13, 141, 144,
154–55; of God, 82, 95, 131–32, 139;
as fruit of the Spirit, 149
Lüdemann, G., 26
Lührmann, D., 26
Luther, M., 82

# Scripture Index